THE KING HAS COME

Dr. James Montgomery Boice was the pastor of the Tenth Presbyterian Church, Philadelphia. In addition to his congregational work, he taught on the 'Bible Study Hour' international radio broadcasts and was a well-known conference speaker. A former chairman of the International Council on Biblical Inerrancy and was a founding member of the Alliance of Confessing Evangelicals. He was a prolific author who wrote over fifty books including Bible commentaries, doctrinal studies and devotional themes. He passed away in 2000 at the age of 61.

THE KING HAS COME

THE REAL MESSAGE OF CHRISTMAS

James Montgomery Boice

CHRISTIAN
FOCUS

ISBN 1-84550-366-X
ISBN 978-1-84550-366-6

© James Montgomery Boice

10 9 8 7 6 5 4 3 2

First published in 1992
Reprinted in 1995 and 2008
by
Christian Focus Publications Ltd
Geanies House, Fearn, Ross-shire,
IV20 1TW, Scotland, Great Britain.

www.christianfocus.com

Cover design by Daniel Van Straaten

Printed by CPD Wales

CONTENTS

To our
Wonderful Counsellor
Mighty God, Everlasting Father
Prince of Peace

PREFACE

About ten years ago I added to my regular output of substantial Bible study books a short collection of Christmas sermons that I had written over the years I had been preaching at Tenth Presbyterian Church in Philadelphia. They were published by Moody Press in Chicago, and they were very well received. One hundred thousand copies were sold in the first three months, and the next year Billy Graham offered the book over the air to supporters of 'The Hour of Decision'. Therefore, when I learned of the interest of the editors of Christian Focus Publications in a new but similar collection, I was delighted to respond with the messages appearing in this volume.

These studies range over the entire Bible, starting with Genesis, but they focus on the birth accounts in Matthew's and Luke's gospels, as one would expect of Christmas sermons. As far as dates go, the sermons were preached in Philadelphia during or near the Christian seasons of 1983 to 1990.

Why should anyone want to publish a book of Christmas sermons?

Why indeed! Christmas is the season of the year in which believers in Jesus Christ from around the world mark the greatest of all the Bible's miracles, namely, the taking upon himself of a true human nature and body by the second person of the holy Trinity. The proper term for this miracle is the Incarnation, and it is this doctrine that stands at the very heart of Christianity. No other religion has at its core the person of one who himself is both fully God and fully man. Even more significant is the fact that no other religion has as its chief doctrine the claim that in the person of this unique God-man, God himself paid the price of our salvation by dying to save us from our many sins.

A religion like this might seem to be inexplicably mysterious, obscure, hard to figure out. And it is true that these doctrines are beyond our full human understanding. Yet this does not mean that Christianity (or Christmas itself) is unfathomable.

It has its mysteries: the Incarnation, the Virgin Birth, the amazing love of God for rebellious human beings. I deal with these and other mysteries in the present volume. I even ask (and answer) the question: Isn't the whole thing absurd?

But the message of Christmas is not only mysterious and puzzling. It is also profoundly simple and appealing, as people of all races and backgrounds have recognized now for nearly two thousand happy years. It tells of a humble couple who wanted only that the will of God should be done in their lives, the birth of a baby in a stable when the parents could find no space in the crowed inn of Bethlehem, the visits of poor shepherds and of rich and distinguished Wise Men, and, most beautiful of all, the announcement of the angel to the shepherds, which was at the same time also an announcement for all persons:

'Do not be afraid. I bring you good news of great joy that will be for all the people. Today in the town of David a Saviour has been born to you; he is Christ the Lord. This will be a sign to you: You will find a baby wrapped in cloths and lying in a manger.'

This was followed by the appearance of a great company of angels, who praised God, saying,

'Glory to God in the highest,
   and on earth peace to men on whom his favour
   rests' (Luke 2:10-14).

That day, so many hundreds of years ago, was the greatest day in history. It was the day of God's favour. It was the climax of Old Testament prophecy and a revelation of God's amazing grace. But today is still the day of God's favour. It is a day in which this identical message is being proclaimed, indeed, it is being proclaimed throughout the entire world. It is a day in which many persons are being drawn to faith in Jesus Christ as Saviour and Lord by God's grace.

I trust that this small book of Christmas messages may be used by God to bring to many people the peace that the incarnation and death of Jesus Christ has made possible.

A word about the title. The publishers are calling this collection *The King Has Come*. It is a good title, because the King of all kings and Lord of all lords has indeed come. That is what Christmas is about. But this will be of no account to you unless the King also comes to you. It is my earnest prayer that he may come to you, perhaps for the first time or in a fresh way, as once again with me you think through these splendid Bible stories.

James Montgomery Boice
Philadelphia, Pennsylvania

Part One

The Prophecies

1

CHRISTMAS IN EDEN[1]

(Genesis 3:15)

And I will put enmity
> between you and the woman,
> and between your offspring and hers;
he will crush your head,
> and you will strike his heel.

If the birth of Jesus Christ, together with his death and resurrection, is the most important event in history and the very heart of the Bible, as Christians believe it is, then we should expect to find this event throughout Scripture. We should find it in the Old Testament as well as in the New, in Genesis as well as Revelation. And we do. The last telling of the Christmas story is in Revelation 12. The first is as early as the third chapter of the book of Genesis. The setting is the Garden of Eden.

Yet Christmas in Eden is still surprising.

Not because the birth of Christ is announced there – we should expect that, as I said – but because of the context.

---

[1] Parts of this study are borrowed with changes from 'The First Messianic Prophecy' in James Montgomery Boice, *Genesis: An Expositional Commentary*, vol 1, Genesis 1:1–11:32 (Grand Rapids: Zondervan Publishing House, 1982), pp. 161-165.

The context is the occasion of God's judgment upon Adam and Eve for their sin.

The devil had come to Eve in the Garden and had tempted her to rebel against God: first, by doubting his benevolence (the devil had suggested that God did not have Adam and Eve's best interests at heart since he had forbidden them to eat from the tree that was in the midst of the Garden); second, by challenging God's word ('You will not surely die,' Gen. 3:4); and third, by dangling before Eve the promise that she and her husband could become 'like God, knowing good and evil' (v. 5). Eve listened to Satan, began to doubt God, and then rebelled against her Creator by eating the fruit of the tree of the knowledge of good and evil. She then gave some to Adam, who ate also.

God came to the Garden to demand an accounting and to pronounce judgment upon our first parents for their sin. How afraid they must have been! Earlier in the story God had told them, 'You are free to eat from any tree in the garden; but you must not eat from the tree of the knowledge of good and evil, for when you eat of it you will surely die' (Gen. 2:16-17). Adam and Eve might not have known what death was in those early days, but the words of God were clearly a formidable threat affixed to a solemn prohibition. And they had done what God had told them not to do! They had eaten from the tree. And now God had come to mete out judgment. By any rational measure they must have expected to die, whatever that might be.

Instead, God pronounced only a token judgment. The woman would have pain in childbirth and would struggle with her husband for supremacy. The man would earn his living with difficulty and in the end return to the dust from which he came. But then – this is the wonderful and utterly unexpected part – God promised them a Deliverer. He promised Jesus, who would come from the woman as her offspring.

The words are part of God's judgment upon Satan since they are a promise of the defeat of him who had been the instrument of Adam and Eve's fall:

And I will put enmity
  between you and the woman,
  and between your offspring and hers;
he will crush your head,
  and you will strike his heel.

Isn't that surprising? It should be. This is the first appearance of grace, the undeserved favour of God, in the Bible, and grace is always surprising.

Christmas is the most surprising grace of all.

Spiritual Warfare

At first glance this verse does not seem particularly wonderful, however. This is because it is speaking about conflict, conflict between Satan and the woman, between his offspring and hers, and between himself and her great descendant, who is Jesus: and conflict does not strike us as wonderful. The word used in the text is 'enmity'.

How can enmity be gracious? How can warfare be wonderful?

The context explains this for us.

We must remember that Satan had rebelled against God earlier. He was the most exalted of the angels. But he was unsatisfied with his position and set his heart, mind, soul and strength on displacing God as ruler of the universe. He was unsuccessful in this rebellion, as we know. He was cast down from his high position. But now he had appeared on earth to do two things. First, he wanted to draw Adam and Eve away from God by causing them to break God's law and bring the judgment of God upon them, as it had fallen on himself. Second, he wanted to get Adam and Eve to follow him. Though the text does not say so explicitly, Satan surely wanted to win the allegiance of our first parents for himself. He succeeded in his first objective. He got Adam and Eve to sin. But he was unsuccessful in his second objective, which is what this important text explains.

It is significant that these words were spoken to Satan. For the new element is not Satan's hatred of Eve. He had hated our first parents from the moment of their creation. It was why he had come to try to draw them away from God. The new thing was to be Eve's and Adam's and all their offspring's hatred of Satan. Not perfectly, to be sure, for they were now sinners themselves. But enough for them not to be drawn automatically into Satan's camp and follow him wholeheartedly.

Suppose God had not created enmity between Satan and the woman. In that case Adam and Eve would have become like Satan (not 'like God'), and from that time forward they would have seen everything from Satan's warped and inverted perspective. That is, they would have considered God to be the utterly evil one and Satan to be the saviour. They would have loved evil and have hated virtue. They would have called truth falsehood and falsehood truth.

In the first chapter of Romans the Apostle Paul says that that is the final and inevitable outcome of suppressing the knowledge of God and going in our own way. But it is at the end of a long line of rebellious acts and does not come immediately or inevitably to everyone. Thus, although the human race is terribly corrupt and although all its ideas of truth and falsehood, right and wrong, are corrupted, human beings nevertheless retain some idea of right and wrong and – this is the important thing – they approve of the good (or think they should) and oppose evil.

That is what Genesis 3:15 speaks of as a first great blessing of God to fallen humanity. When we sin, we find that we like sin and only want to escape its consequences. But God has so ordered things that sin brings misery and we are therefore unable to lie down in it and love it completely. We would like to go to hell happy. But one aspect of grace is that God does not allow that to happen. God has created enmity between ourselves and Satan, which limits the hold sin has on us and makes it possible for us to hear God's voice and respond to him, in spite of our misery.

The Two Humanities

There is a second antagonism in these verses, and this is between the descendants of Satan and the descendants of the woman. This has been thought of as a conflict between the demons and people. But that is probably not what the verse is about, simply because the demons are independently created beings and are not Satan's 'offspring', as we are offspring of our parents. The conflict is actually between the godly descendants of the woman, who follow her and Adam in believing God and thus being influenced by him, and the ungodly descendants of the woman, who do not submit to God and thus continue to be influenced by Satan. We find this distinction, a distinction between what has been called the two humanities, in Genesis 4 and 5.

Is this good?

It certainly is. For the warfare between those who are attempting to follow God and those who are following Satan causes the godly to draw close to God and depend upon God, which is a blessing. Isaac Watts, one of the greatest hymn writers in the English language, wrote a hymn, *Am I a soldier of the cross*, which has the stanza,

Are there no foes for me to face?
    Must I not stem the flood?
Is this vile world a friend of grace,
    To help me on to God?

17

In the context of the hymn the answer to that last question is clearly No. This world is no friend of ours. It is our enemy. Watts is encouraging us to fight on against the world for Jesus' sake. But in the context of what we are finding in Genesis there is a sense in which the world is a friend of grace, for its very hatred pushes the righteous to a greater dependence upon God.

Our hatred of Satan and the world's hatred of us are two great Christmas gifts. They were the first ever given.

Christ's Victory at the Cross

Yet neither would be effective in the end if it were not for the third gift predicted in this passage. It is the chief reason for the verse, for what it promises is a Deliverer from God who would be born of the woman. It is a prediction of the birth, yes, even the Virgin Birth of Christ. Since this is the first promise of the coming of Christ in the Bible, Genesis 3:15 has been called the *protoevangelion*, that is, the first announcement of the Christian gospel.

But notice: this too is a struggle. More than that, it is deadly warfare. For in this case the battle is not described as antagonism only but as a fight to the finish in which, on the one hand, the Deliverer is to be wounded in the heel by Satan but in which, on the other hand, Jesus is to destroy the devil by crushing his head.

At first, the birth of Jesus to Mary seemed to play into the devil's hand. For as long as the Trinity remained enthroned in heaven in full possession of the divine glory and power, God was unassailable to Satan. He could not touch him. But as soon as Jesus was born to Mary, God came, so it seemed, within his adversary's grasp. Probably the devil worked upon Joseph's mind as soon as he discovered Mary's pregnancy, causing him to suspect her of fornication. It required a visit by an angel to assure Joseph that Mary had not been unfaithful but was with child by the Holy Spirit. Later, we can be sure, Satan worked on the mind of King Herod to cause him to lash out against the supposed pretender to his throne, even though Jesus was just a child at the time. Herod's enmity resulted in the murder of the infants of Bethlehem. But Jesus, Mary and Joseph escaped to Egypt, having been warned by God in a dream of Herod's plot.

When Jesus grew to manhood and was ready to begin his public ministry Satan struck again. He confronted Jesus in the wilderness and tried to turn him aside from the path God had marked out for him. He tried to get him to doubt the Word of God, just as he had tried and succeeded in getting Adam and Eve to doubt God and then to rebel against him. But Jesus defeated Satan by applying the sword of the Spirit, which is Scripture.

Satan's hatred of Christ erupted again and again throughout his earthly life and ministry.

On one occasion Satan tried to destroy Jesus in a storm. But Jesus arose and rebuked the wind and waves, causing them to become calm.

On another occasion Satan moved the citizens of Nazareth to try to murder Jesus by throwing him off a high cliff.

Sometimes the devil got people to pick up stones to stone him.

When he was unsuccessful with the masses of the people Satan whipped up the hatred of the religious leaders, who plotted against Jesus, tried to catch him in some crime punishable by death, and sent soldiers to arrest him. The hatred of the leaders was that of the carnal mind which is enmity against God. They had shown their hatred of the former prophets. Now they were trying to kill God's Son. Jesus described these men in the parable of the tenants who killed the messengers and then, when the owner of the land sent his only son, cried, 'This is the heir; come, let's kill him, and take his inheritance' (Matt. 1:38).

Satan's plots against Jesus were many, shrewd and various. But Jesus always escaped unhurt. He was master of every situation.

Yet Satan is no quitter, and he certainly did not quit now. Instead he kept working closer and closer to Jesus and finally succeeded in penetrating into his inner circle. He entered the heart of Judas and moved him to betray his Master.

Thus the events of the final day unfolded: the arrest of Jesus by night, the hastily-arranged trial before the Jewish Sanhedrin, the appearance before Pilate, the flogging, the sentence of death, the walk to Golgotha, finally the pounding of the nails into the flesh and the crucifixion.

I do not know what was going through Satan's mind in that moment, but he must have overflowed with glee. At last he had succeeded. God had been so foolish as to come within his grasp, and Satan had accomplished at last what he would have given anything and everything to accomplish: the murder of God. Satan must have clasped his hands triumphantly. But in that moment of apparent victory he must have forgotten the prophecy spoken in the Garden of Eden, the prophecy which said the coming one would be bruised by Satan but would at the same time crush his head. Satan had succeeded in bruising God. But it was only a bruising, not a defeat. On the third day Jesus rose from the tomb triumphantly.

And as for Satan? He was destroyed, even though he did not know it at the time. He failed to see that his victory was only a Pyrrhic victory and his triumph only a momentary triumph. Dr. John H. Gerstner wrote of this triumph, 'Satan was majestically triumphant in this ... battle. He had nailed Jesus to the cross. The prime object of all his striving through all the ages was achieved. But he had failed. For the prophecy which had said that he would indeed bruise the seed of the woman had also said that his head would be crushed by Christ's heel. Thus, while Satan was celebrating his triumph in battle over the Son of God, the full weight of the Atonement accomplished by the Crucifixion (which the devil had effected) came down on him, and he realised that all this time, so far from successfully battling against the Almighty, he had actually been carrying out the purposes of the all-wise God.'[2]

What Satan had failed to see is that his only true power – unlike his pretensions to power – comes from God, particularly from God's character. He knows that God is holy, and rightly surmised that God must punish sin. He thought that if he could get our first parents to sin, the holy wrath of God against sin would come down on them. God's good purposes for men and women would be thwarted. What Satan did not know (and no one could know fully until Jesus actually died for us) is how God could be both just in punishing sin and merciful in saving sinners. The devil failed to understand how much God loved Adam and Eve, how Jesus had been sent by God to bear sin's punishment and that his own power would be broken in the process.

Faith Only

Satan did not understand what was to happen by the Atonement, and no one did understand it fully until the death of Jesus Christ, as I said. Yet the godly who lived before the coming of Christ did understand it, at least to some degree, and they believed on the one who was promised.

Adam believed on Jesus!
And so did Eve!

---

[2] John H Gerstner, 'The Language of the Battlefield' in *Our Saviour God: Studies on Man, Christ and the Atonement*, ed. by James Montgomery Boice (Grand Rapids: Baker Book House, 1980), pp. 159, 160.

The reason I say that Adam believed on Jesus is because of Genesis 3:20, in which he names his wife Eve. People sometimes suppose that God named the woman Eve, just as he named the man Adam. But that is not the case. God named the couple Mr. and Mrs. Adam (cf. Gen. 5:2), and the woman is not named Eve in the story before this point. She was called Eve by Adam. But why? The answer is in the meaning of the name. Eve means 'life' or 'life-giver', and the reason Adam called the woman Eve is because of the promise we are studying.

Adam must have been thinking along these lines: 'God warned us that we were going to die if we ate from the tree of the knowledge of good and evil. We did eat of it, and we should die. But we have not died. God came in judgment, and although we are going to have a much harder time of it from now on, death has at least been postponed. Besides, God has promised a Deliverer to come, a Deliverer who is going to be bruised for us. I suppose this means that he will suffer death in our place, and while he is doing that he will destroy Satan and his works. Moreover, that Deliverer is going to be born of you, Eve, for God called him your offspring. I believe that, and in order to show I believe it I am going to call you 'Life-giver'. You are going to give birth, and the one who will be born of you will be the Saviour.'

And it was not only Adam who believed the promise God gave in the Garden on that first Christmas. Eve believed it too. For when the child was born – we read about it in Genesis 4 – she called him Cain, which means 'Acquired' or 'Here he is!' She was mistaken in thinking that the child she held in her arms was the Deliverer. She was not holding Jesus but rather the world's first murderer. But she had the right idea. She was looking ahead to the one who should be born, and she was staking her life on the reliability and truth of God's promise.

So have all who have understood what Christmas is all about. And so must you, if you are to be a true part of it.

Christmas is not about trees, and tinsel, and gifts, and angels, and shepherds, and stars, and Wise Men, though some of those things enter into the New Testament story. Christmas is about a Deliverer from sin, promised to our first parents by God thousands of years ago in Eden. They had sinned and would have perished in their transgression. But God said that he was going to send his own Son, the Lord Jesus Christ, to save them from it. And God did. The Bible says, 'But when the time had fully come, God sent his son, born of a woman, born under law, to redeem those under law, that we might receive the full rights of sons' (Gal. 4:4-5).

The carols proclaim it. For example,

God rest you merry gentlemen,
Let nothing you dismay.
Remember Christ our Saviour
Was born on Christmas day,
To save us all from Satan's power
When we were gone astray.
O tidings of comfort and joy, comfort and joy,
O tidings of comfort and joy.

Make sure that these are your glad tidings. Make sure that you also trust in Jesus as your Saviour, as Eve and Adam, and all God's people from all ages of the history of the world, have before you.

2

FOUR GIFTS FOR CHRISTMAS

(Isaiah 9:6)

For to us a child is born,
to us a son is given,
and the government will be on his shoulders.
And he will be called
Wonderful Counsellor, Mighty God,
Everlasting Father, Prince of Peace.

This chapter is about 'four gifts of Christmas', which means that if it were not for the text printed above, anyone merely reading the title would most naturally think about the Wise Men. And since the Wise Men of the Bible brought three gifts – gold, incense, and myrrh – the reader would probably expect the study to be about the so-called 'other Wise Man'. As far as I know, this man, if he existed, did not bring anything according to that extra-biblical story. But presumably there would have been a gift, and his gift together with the other three would make four. Many sermons have probably been preached along those lines.

But that is not what I am thinking about. I am thinking instead of the great text in the ninth chapter of Isaiah in which the coming of the Lord Jesus Christ and the nature of his anticipated ministry are spelled out in four great phrases, which are also his names: Wonderful Counsellor, Mighty God, Everlasting Father, Prince of Peace.

The verse is a birth announcement. But it is strikingly different from any other birth announcement that has ever been made by any parent. This birth announcement was issued before the child was born. If you pay attention to birth announcements, you may have noticed that they come in a variety of styles and wordings, and sometimes they are quite late. I have received all kinds. But never in my life have I received a birth announcement before the child was born. Even when people know whether they are going to have a boy or a girl, as is possible today, the announcement always comes afterwards. But here is an announcement of the birth of God's Son made hundreds of years before the incarnation.

The first part of this verse anticipates Christ's dual nature when it speaks of a 'child' being 'born' and a 'son' being 'given.' Jesus was not born as a Son, because he already was a Son. He was the eternal Son of God, the second person of the Godhead. As the Son he was given. But Jesus was born as a child, which is a way of describing the incarnation, in which the divine Son of God took on human nature. It teaches that the second person of the Godhead became a man. Isaiah may not have understood that fully himself. But we can see how the language of the text, guided by the Holy Spirit, prophetically announced Christ's two natures.

What I am particularly interested in here, however, are the four names for Jesus that occur in the second half of the verse. They are great names, for they describe who this incarnate Son of God is, and they do so in terms of his gifts to us. By describing him as a Wonderful Counsellor, the verse tells us that he is the source of divine spiritual wisdom, which we need. By calling him the Mighty

God, it tells us that he will empower us for life's tasks. Everlasting Father unfolds the gift of sonship. Prince of Peace highlights the gifts of peace both between ourselves and God, and internally.

What do you do when a baby is born? If you are close to the family, you bring a gift. But here is a case in which the child himself brings gifts – because of who he is and what he came to do.

Wonderful Counsellor

The first name for Jesus is Wonderful Counsellor. This has to do with wisdom, because wisdom is what a counsellor provides. I am glad those two words are put together in the *New International Version*, for this is certainly an improvement over the versions we are most used to hearing. When we hear these terms, I suppose most of us have Handel's *Messiah* in mind. Or if not, we are certainly familiar with the *King James Bible*, where there is a comma between the words 'Wonderful' and 'Counsellor'. The way the *King James Bible* reads, it sounds as if there are five titles for our Lord. He is to be called: (1) Wonderful, (2) Counsellor, followed by (3) Mighty God, (4) Everlasting Father and (5) Prince of Peace. I think the modern translations are better – certainly the parallelism is intact – when 'Wonderful' is linked to 'Counsellor' and the first name becomes a combination of the two terms.

We have a great need in this area, because we all lack wisdom. Or, to push it back even further, we lack knowledge of all the important spiritual things. It is possible, of course, to receive a good education and learn a great deal about a great many things and so become, in the opinion of this world, quite learned men and women – and yet to lack knowledge of what really matters in this life.

Think of all the educated people of the world who cannot answer a simple question like, Who am I? They spend a great deal of time trying to find answers to that question, usually without success. Or how about, Why am I here? Is there a meaning to my life? Is there anything greater than or beyond myself? Is there a God? Is there a goal to history? Is there something that I am made to fit into?

Apart from the revelation that God provides, there are no answers to questions like that. But in Jesus Christ we find the beginning of wisdom in the gift of such knowledge.

It is in Christ that we find who God is. He said, 'Anyone who has seen me has seen the Father' (John 14:9). So if you want to know who God is and what God is like, the answer has been provided. God is like Jesus.

It is in Christ that we also find out who we are. We are sinful men and women, and we know this in part because when we come to know Jesus we discover that we are not like him. He is the holy One; we are not holy. At the same time and in spite of that, we learn that we are valuable in God's sight and are loved by him – so valuable, in fact, and so loved, that God sent Jesus Christ, his Son, to die for us. It is in Christ that we find both our sinfulness and our value as beings made in God's image.

Do I have a purpose in life? I also find the answer to that question in Jesus Christ, because he provides it when he says, 'Come, follow me.' Our purpose is to become his disciples. What is more, he tells us what he is going to do with us when we do come to him. He is going to make us fishers of men. He is going to send us out into the world with this gospel so that through our witness – not by a revelation brought by an angel, but through our witness – other people are going to hear about him and become Christians too. We have been given this great task. So what we say, how we live and what we do in life become important.

And yet, the name Wonderful Counsellor goes beyond even these things I have mentioned, because it is possible to have a great deal of knowledge and yet not know what to do with it.

As I grow older, I am particularly conscious of this in relation to the ministry. There is a sense in which, when a young man goes to college and learns the skills he needs to be a minister, he comes fairly well equipped for the task. (At least a minister should come equipped for the task.) So he applies the skills and begins to get on with the work of teaching the Bible and pastoring a church. But there comes a point – at least, it has for me – when the minister begins to see that what he most needs is wisdom. He knows certain things. He knows how to do a job. But what precisely should he do? How should he apply what he has?

Here is where the Lord Jesus Christ has a special ministry to us. He had it for the disciples in their day. He was teaching them, yes, and they were learning a great deal from him. But what he was really doing was imparting divine or spiritual wisdom to them.

Moreover, when he was about to be taken out of the world, he turned to these very men and gave a great promise. He said, 'I am going to be taken from you, but I am going to send someone to be with you, for ever be to you what I am. His name is *Paracletos*.' This word is translated 'Comforter' or 'Advocate' in our Bibles, which is a very good indication of what the Greek word means. An 'advocate' is a person who is called alongside another to help, which is the exact meaning of the Greek word: 'one called alongside of to help'. Moreover, this is the role of a counsellor in the legal sense. Jesus helped us while he was here. But now that he has returned to the Father he has sent the Paraclete, a wise Counsellor who explains, on the one hand, what God the Father wants for us so we might begin to understand it and grow in that direction, and, on the other hand, takes our requests and interprets them properly before the Father.

When Jesus came to earth he came as a Wonderful Counsellor, and when he returned to heaven he did not leave us without wisdom. He provided what we need.

James talks about it. He says, 'If any of you lacks wisdom, he should ask God, who gives generously to all without finding fault, and it will be given to him' (Jas. 1:5). In that same chapter he says, 'Every good and perfect gift is from above' (v. 17). So if you value wisdom and you ask God for it, he will give it to you. It comes through Jesus Christ.

The Mighty God
The second great gift that is mentioned in Isaiah 9:6 is power, because Jesus is called 'the Mighty God'. That is, the most mighty God, the powerful God.

A lot of people are 'into' power today, as we say. So power is not a hard concept for us to understand. People are very conscious of power, whether they have it or whether they don't. People high up in business are regarded as having power. They may feel they have less of it when they get it than people who are looking at them imagine, but we still think of power as being associated with a high position on the organisational chart.

Or we think of power in terms of money. If we have enough money, we have power. Money enables us to control circumstances to an extent.

Or we think of power in politics. If you get into an elected position in our governmental system, then you have power. We speak of 'empowering people, empowering the masses, empowering minorities,' because the weak and the poor often lack adequate representation. We say, 'Well, if only we can get them organised so they can vote and elect a proper representative, then they will be empowered.' We even say that at some level or another everybody needs to have some power which, if put in other terms, simply means that they need to be in control of their lives.

But the tragedy at this point is that in an age which, perhaps more than any other, has been conscious of power, we are actually conscious of the opposite, that is, of being powerless. We feel that we have no ability really to change events. We see this in national elections. One of the most puzzling things about American democracy is that at the time of an election so few citizens who are qualified to vote actually exercise that franchise. In recent years the figure is only about thirty-five percent. Why? People reply that 'it doesn't make a difference.' And maybe they're right. But whether they are right or wrong, when they say, 'It wouldn't make a difference,' and don't vote as a result, what they are really saying is, 'I don't have power to control my own destiny.' We talk about empowerment. We want to empower other people, but we ourselves feel unable to control anything.

The fact that Jesus Christ is the Mighty God speaks a timely word to us in this area. Since Jesus is the Mighty God, in giving us Jesus God shows that he is himself on our side and is empowering us. He demonstrated that by Jesus' death. Why would Jesus die for us if he didn't care for us? Why would he go to all that trouble, all that suffering, if he didn't intend to rescue us from our sin and make us to become sons of God? He also shows it by the gift of the Holy Spirit, which is the means by which Jesus, the Mighty God, comes to be with us and live in us.

I notice in the Christmas story that when the characters involved speak about the meaning of these events, as Mary does in her *Magnificat*, what they talk about are the mighty acts of God on our behalf. They remind themselves how God came in power to deliver his people from Egypt, how he drove their enemies from the land of promise, and how he kept them there year after year. That is our God too, and what he has done for others, he will do for us. In different ways, of course. We have different problems; and God has different goals for us than he had for the ancient Jewish people. But the power of that mighty God is ours also.

The early disciples knew that they had power. The Lord said to them in one version of the Great Commission, 'You will receive power when the Holy Spirit comes on you; and you will be my witnesses in Jerusalem, and in all Judea and Samaria, and to the ends of the earth' (Acts 1:8). And they said, 'Amen. If that is what God says, if we are to receive power and be his witnesses, then we will be his witnesses.' So with that message and that assurance they went out, preached the gospel, won many to Christ and literally transformed the world.

Do you feel sometimes – I know I do – that what we do doesn't really make a difference? We feel that we are easily replaced. Or that what we do is soon forgotten. Or that trying to do the right thing or live a moral life doesn't influence anybody. The early Christians did not feel that. They knew that what they were doing did make a difference, because, I suppose more than we do, they had a sense of what the world is without Jesus Christ. They knew how grim life can be. When we get bogged down in the little worries of our lives, we lose this big picture and fail to appreciate the difference Jesus makes.

Perhaps at Christmas especially, even more than at other times, we need to recapture what it is to have the Mighty God as our God and know that we actually can make a difference in the power of the Holy Spirit. Do you believe that? If you do, then you will not hesitate to speak about the Lord. You will not say, 'But people will laugh at me.' You will speak about Jesus, because you will know that God is going to bless your witness and use it to bring others to faith.

Everlasting Father
The third of these four terms is Everlasting Father. One thing it teaches is the deity of Jesus. 'Mighty God' does that, too, of course, but it is particularly striking, that, when God is announcing the coming of his Son to be the Saviour, he gives him the title 'Father'. We ourselves make a distinction between God the Father and God the Son. But here God the Father is calling his Son the Everlasting Father. This is not meant to blur the distinctions between the persons of the Son and Father, of course. But it is a way of saying, 'Everything that I am, my Son is.' And, of course, that is just good theology.

However, when we are approaching these names in terms of God's gifts to us through Jesus Christ, what this term really talks about is our becoming members of God's family. It speaks of belonging. Apart from the work of Jesus and the gifts of God to us in him, we do not belong spiritually. We are outside, alienated from God. But through the work of Jesus Christ in paying the penalty for our sins by dying for them, and by the work of the Holy Spirit in bringing us to faith, we who were outside are now brought near and made a part of God's great family.

There are many great privileges in that.

One privilege is that we can now come to God, not as aliens but as sons and daughters. So we are encouraged to pray, knowing that our heavenly Father understands us, loves us, cares for us and encourages us to lay our requests before him. Furthermore, he promises to answer our prayers in perfect love and according to his own wise purposes for us.

Are you discouraged? Tell God about it. Say, 'Oh, Father, I am so discouraged. What I am doing is so difficult. I have been working away at this thing, and I seem to be getting nowhere.' Ask for encouragement, and you will find that God gives it.

Are you defeated? You can take your defeats to God too. Say, 'I have lost this battle, and I don't think I can get up and get going again. Help me.' You will find that the God of resurrections will renew your strength and give you new energy. Remember that Jesus taught his disciples to call God 'Father', using the special word abba, which means 'daddy'. Because of Jesus' work, those who believe on him can have an intimate, not a distant, relationship with the Father.

Prince of Peace

The fourth gift of Christmas, embodied in the fourth name for Jesus in Isaiah 9:6, is peace. Jesus is the Prince of Peace. I suppose that of all the things men and women lack today, peace is the most notable lack, for we live in a restless age. If we should ask people, 'What is it you most want in life?' they would probably answer in a lot of different ways. But if we probe beneath the surface, I am sure we would find that what men and women want more than anything else is to be at peace. We are not at peace. We are not at peace with God, which is our fundamental problem.

St. Augustine understood this well. He said, 'Our hearts are restless until they rest in thee.'

Actually, apart from the work of Jesus Christ on our behalf and faith in him, we are at war with God. We are fighting God with all our heart, mind, soul and strength, because what we want to be is God in our own lives. We want to determine our own destinies. Jesus overcame this enmity by his death for us. He bridged the gap, making peace between God and those who were hostile to him.

Now, having been given peace with God, we are also given that other great blessing, the peace of God, which is given to all who are in Jesus Christ and ask God for it.

'Do not be anxious about anything, but in everything, by prayer and petition, with thanksgiving, present your requests to God. And the peace of God, which transcends all understanding, will guard your hearts and your minds in Christ Jesus' (Phil. 4:6, 7). Isn't it wonderful to know that we can have the peace of God in Jesus Christ as one of God's great gifts?

As I think about these gifts, I am impressed at how well they correspond to the needs of the human heart. Suppose, even apart from the biblical revelation, that we should conduct an opinion poll to find out what men and women feel they most need. Suppose we should ask, 'What do you feel are your greatest needs?'

'Well,' people would say, 'we have minds. So we have a need to know things rightly, to understand. We need wisdom. We also have wills, and because we have wills we want to achieve something. We want our lives to make a difference. To do that we need power. We are also individuals, but we sense that we are not meant to be alone. We want to belong somewhere. We need satisfying relationships. We are also conscious of having done wrong things. We need to be forgiven. We need somebody to deal with our guilt.' Isn't that what we would find if we should poll people and analyse their basic experiences? Aren't those the things we really need?

As I look at these gifts, I find that they speak to each of those needs.

To know the truth! Jesus Christ is the truth, and he is for us a Wonderful Counsellor.

To achieve something worthwhile! Jesus is the Mighty God who enables us to do that. We accomplish worthwhile things through his power.

To belong to someone! Jesus answers this need, because he is our Everlasting Father. Through him we are brought into God's family.

To be forgiven and be at peace! Jesus is the Prince of Peace. He has made peace for us by his death.

Four gifts for Christmas. They are the greatest gifts that anybody can give or we can have, and they are all in Jesus. They are for us. They are for you, if you will have them.

3

A Mighty Ruler from a Little Town

(Micah 5:2)

But you, Bethlehem Ephrathah,
    though you are small among the clans of Judah,
out of you will come for me
    one who will be ruler over Israel,
whose origins are from of old,
    from ancient times.

When the Wise Men came to Jerusalem in the early months following the birth of Jesus Christ, they asked to see the new king, and those who heard the Magi's questions were disturbed – particularly King Herod. It was because Judea already had a king, and Herod was that king. Herod was also a crafty old politician, and he knew danger when he saw it. He did not know who this king was, but that did not mean that no king existed. Herod set about to find where this 'pretender' was so that he might kill him.

Who would know about his birth-place?

If anyone would know, it would be the chief priests and teachers of the law. So Herod called them together and asked where the child was to be born.

The rulers did not hesitate for a moment. They knew the answer to that question. It must have been on every 'trivia question' list in Jerusalem. The answer was in Micah 5:2. So they answered immediately,

> 'In Bethlehem of Judea, for this is what the prophet has written:
> "But you, Bethlehem, in the land of Judah,
>   are by no means least among the rulers of Judah;
>   for out of you will come a ruler
>   who will be the shepherd of my people Israel"'
>   (Matt. 2:5, 6)

The interesting thing about this reply is that in spite of their knowledge of the text and their awareness of the Wise Men's question, with all it implied regarding the birth of their Messiah, none of the Jewish leaders took time to investigate the reports of this anticipated birth for themselves. They had an interest in the case. He was their Messiah, after all. His birth and the announcement of the place of his birth was in their Scriptures. But it was as true of them then as Jesus later declared it to be of them and others during his ministry, that they diligently studied the Scriptures yet would not come to him that they might have life (John 5:39-40).

The Magi went to Bethlehem and found Jesus. But these rulers were too busy or too lazy or too unconcerned to make the short trip. Bethlehem is only five miles south of Jerusalem along what was even then a well-built and well-travelled road. But these leaders of Israel would not inconvenience themselves even a little bit to go and find him.

A Little Town with a Great History
In the modern state of Israel Bethlehem is not a very big town even today, and it was much smaller at the time of Jesus' birth. Still, although it was small – the text says,

'small among the clans of Judah' – it had a long and illustrious history.

The first biblical mention of Bethlehem is in Genesis 35, a chapter that contains one of the most poignant stories in that book. Jacob, the grandson of Abraham, was on his way to Hebron from Bethel, after his return from living in Mesopotamia with his uncle Laban, and he paused on the way to Bethlehem because his beloved wife Rachel, for whom he had worked fourteen years, was giving birth and was having trouble in her labour. A son was born. Jacob named him Benjamin. But Rachel died, and the loss was so great to Jacob that years later, when he was blessing Manasseh and Ephraim, the sons of Joseph, Jacob paused in his blessing to reminisce sorrowfully: ' "As I was returning from Paddan, to my sorrow Rachel died in the land of Canaan while we were still on the way, a little distance from Ephrath. So I buried her there beside the road to Ephrath" (that is, Bethlehem)' (Gen. 48:7).

This first mention of Bethlehem identifies it as a place of sadness, as the burial place of Jacob's wife, Rachel.

Caleb, a hero of the Jewish conquest of Canaan under Joshua, was also linked to Bethlehem, because it lay in the territory he claimed as his inheritance (Josh. 14:12-15; 1 Chron. 2:24, 51, 54). Caleb's second wife was called Ephrath (1 Chron. 2:19), perhaps giving her name to this city, for at one time Bethlehem was called by a combination of his and her names: 'Caleb Ephrathah' (1 Chron. 2:24).

One of the most beautiful stories of the Old Testament is also set in Bethlehem. It is the story of Ruth. Ruth was a Moabite woman, a foreigner. But when her mother-in-law Naomi returned to her own land to settle in Bethlehem after the death of her husband and two sons, Ruth determined to return with her and settle where she did. 'Don't urge me to leave you or to turn back from you. Where you go I will go, and where you stay I will stay. Your people will be my people and your God my God. Where you die I will die, and there I will be buried' (Ruth 1:16, 17).

In Bethlehem Ruth met Boaz, a wealthy man of the town, and she became his wife. Their son was Obed, who was the father of Jesse, who was the father of King David. The book of Ruth closes by recording this important ancestry, and it was probably included in the Hebrew canon for that specific purpose.

Of course, it is David for whom Bethlehem is chiefly known. 1 Samuel 16 tells how the prophet Samuel went to Bethlehem to anoint a successor to the unworthy King Saul. Jesse produced each of his seven oldest sons, beginning with Eliab, the firstborn, but the Lord passed by each of them until the youngest, David, was eventually brought in from the fields and was chosen. As far as their outward appearances were concerned, the other sons of Jesse seemed to be better choices for a king. But God explained, 'Do not consider [their] appearance or [their] height, for I have rejected [them]. The LORD does not look at the things man looks at. Man looks at the outward appearance, but the LORD looks at the heart' (1 Sam. 16:7).

While Saul reigned as king, David often passed from Saul's encampment to Bethlehem to feed his sheep (1 Sam. 17:15).

David loved the small town and often thought of it. Once, when Bethlehem was occupied by the Philistines, David exclaimed, 'Oh, that someone would get me a drink of water from the well near the gate of Bethlehem' (2 Sam. 23:15). Three of David's mighty men were standing by, heard him speak these words and took his request seriously. Out of the love they had for David they broke through the Philistine lines, drew water from the well and brought it back to him. But David poured it out as an offering to the Lord, saying, 'Far be it from me, O LORD, to do this! Is it not the blood of men who went at the risk of their lives?' (v. 17).

Bethlehem was a small town among the many towns of Judah, but with a great history. And yet, the history of Bethlehem was to become even greater, for it was out of Bethlehem that he who was to be a divine and everlasting ruler over Israel would come.

Out of Bethlehem

How wonderful the way it happened! Joseph, the adoptive father of Jesus, and Mary, his virgin mother, were of Davidic descent. Their ancestral home was Bethlehem. But they did not live in Bethlehem. They lived in Nazareth where Joseph was a carpenter. How could it happen that their son, Jesus, could be born where the prophet said he was to be born – in Bethlehem, so many miles (and so many long days of travel) to the south?

We know how it happened.

The great Caesar Augustus had a quarrel with King Herod and determined that Judea should therefore be taxed as an imperial province instead of existing as a separate kingdom. To accomplish that purpose he determined that everyone should return to the city of his or her ancestors to be registered. So we read in Luke's gospel,

> So Joseph also went up from the town of Nazareth in Galilee to Judea, to Bethlehem the town of David, because he belonged to the house and line of David. He went there to register with Mary, who was pledged to be married to him and was expecting a child (Luke 2:4, 5).

This was a highly unlikely occurrence from a human perspective. Taxation was common enough in antiquity. It has been common at all periods of history, including our own. But registrations of this type were not common. Besides, there was the timing. Luke tells us that it was while Quirinius was governor of Syria (Luke 2:2). Why then? Or why during this precise month? Why at the very time that Mary was nearing the end of her pregnancy and was about to give birth?

Why indeed?

It was so that the Scriptures might be fulfilled and the perfect plan of God in the birth of his Son, our Saviour, might unfold on schedule and in detail. Micah had written, 'But you, Bethlehem Ephrathah ... out of you will come for me one who will be ruler over Israel.'

And so it was!

In his treatment of Micah 5:2, Charles Haddon Spurgeon waxes eloquent at this point, in asking why the taxation came in this precise way. He answers,

> It was Caesar's whim; but it was God's decree. Oh! we love the sublime doctrine of eternal absolute predestination. Some have doubted its being consistent with the free agency of man. We know well it is so, and we never saw any difficulty in the subject; we believe metaphysicians have made difficulties; we see none ourselves. It is for us to believe that man does as he pleases, yet notwithstanding he always does as God decrees. If Judas betrays Christ, 'thereunto he was appointed'; and if Pharaoh hardens his heart, yet 'for this purpose have I raised thee up, for to show forth my power in thee.' Man doth as he wills; but God maketh him to do as he willeth, too ... Everything is of God; and unto him who guideth the stars and wingeth sparrows, who ruleth planets and yet moveth atoms, who speaks thunders and yet whispers zephyrs, unto him be glory; for there is God in everything.[1]

---

[1] Charles Haddon Spurgeon, 'The Incarnation and Birth of Christ', *The New Park Street Pulpit,* vol. 2 (Pasadena, Texas: Pilgrim Publications, 1975), pp. 28, 29.

The birth of Jesus at Bethlehem shows us many things about God, but chief among them is God's eternal, predestinating power. God's choice for the birth-place of his divine Son was Bethlehem. So in Bethlehem the Lord Jesus Christ *was* born.

A Great Ruler over Israel

We come now to the chief part of our text, the last part, which tells us that this prophesied descendant of David was to be no inconsequential person but a 'ruler over Israel'. David was a ruler, of course. So were many of his descendants. But since the fall of Judah to Babylon in 586 BC the house and line of David had fallen on hard times. To say that a descendant of David would be a ruler over Israel was therefore to prophesy a great and important restoration. Moreover, it was a summons to faith, for nothing could have seemed less probable of fulfilment for nearly six long centuries and after many years of Jewish domination by the Romans.

Yet 'when the time had fully come' (Gal. 4:4), God sent his Son to redeem those born under the law and condemned by it, and to rule over them. And he was born in Bethlehem.

There are two reasons why the one prophesied in Micah 5:2 is the one and only legitimate ruler over Israel (and of all other persons too).

First, he is the eternal Son of the eternal God and therefore the only absolute and rightful monarch of anybody. This is what Micah was speaking of when he identified him as he 'whose origins are from of old, from ancient times'. Jesus was to be a true man certainly. He was to be born of a true human mother in King David's kingly line. But he was to be no mere man. He was also to be God of whom alone it can be said, his origins are from 'of old, from ancient times'.

43

Isaiah uttered the same truths in his prophecy:

'For to us a child is born,
  to us a son is given,
  and the government will be on his shoulders.
And he will be called
  Wonderful Counsellor, Mighty God,
  Everlasting Father, Prince of Peace.
Of the increase of his government and peace
  there will be no end.
He will reign on David's throne
  and over his kingdom,
establishing and upholding it
  with justice and righteousness
  from that time on and for ever' (Isa. 9:6, 7).

According to Isaiah, the child to be born should be none less than the 'Mighty God' and the 'Everlasting Father' of all, as improbable as that might have seemed to those who first read his words.

And there is this too. When the Wise Men came to Jerusalem inquiring after the new ruler and were directed to Bethlehem on the basis of Micah's prophecy, they asked for 'the one who has been born king of the Jews' (Matt. 2:2). That is, they were asking for one who was a king from the very moment of his birth.

Have you ever considered how unusual that is? Almost invariably, even though one is born into a royal line and is destined to be a king, it is necessary for the person to wait for the death of the monarch preceding him. It is probably impossible to find a case in all history where any infant was born a king. Yet that was true of Jesus, and the reason it was true is that he already was a king and had been from eternity past. Jesus is the King of all earthly kings, both past and present, for he is the eternal Lord of lords. Remember that the next time you sing:

Born thy people to deliver,
Born a child, and yet a king.

Or when you hear that great chorus from Handel's Messiah:

King of kings and Lord of lords –
Hallelujah!

Remember that when Jesus was born in Bethlehem he came, not only to be a ruler, but as a ruler over Israel. Jesus came as a ruler, because he already was Israel's King.

Second, it is not only his person that establishes Jesus as a ruler. That would be enough in itself. Jesus is God, and God does reign. But in addition, the One who was to be born in Bethlehem (and who was born there on that first Christmas) was also ruler by virtue of his future work. He was to redeem his people, delivering them from the shackles of their sin. Thus, he earned the right (as well as having intrinsically possessed the right) of being their personal and particular King and Lord. Jesus is their ruler because he has purchased a special people for himself by dying for them.

Born In Us

At this point the prophecy of a ruler, given to the Wise Men, becomes quite personal. For the issue is not merely whether the one born in this small Judean town so long ago really was a great ruler, but whether he is your ruler. The question is, Are you his subject? Have you bowed your knee to him in proper homage?

You say, 'I have never bowed before anyone. I run my own life.' If that is so, then you are opposed to Christ, regardless of what sentimental feelings you may or may not have at Christmas time. You are among that rebellious host of Psalm 2, who take their stand against the Lord and his Anointed One, saying, 'Let us break their chains

... and throw off their fetters' (vv. 2, 3). The Bible says that God laughs at such folly and will soon overthrow it. God regards your opposition to the rightful rule of his Son Jesus Christ over you as a matter of personal derision.

Another may say, 'I believe that Jesus is a mighty ruler, even that he is (or may be) God, and I am willing to have him as my Lord someday. But not now, especially not at Christmas. There are so many things to do, so many good times to be had, so many sins to be indulged. I'll come to him later.' If you are saying this, your folly may be even greater than those who would rebel against him entirely, because you are self-deluded. You will never come to him at that rate. Your sins will take you further and further from him, and eventually you will perish.

A third person says, 'But Christ is my Lord. It is just that I want to run my own life now. I want to do what seems best to me to do.' If you are saying that, remember what Jesus said to people who made the same vain profession in his day: 'Why do you call me, "Lord, Lord," and do not do what I say?' (Luke 6:46). According to Jesus, those who go their way, rather than his, are not his true disciples. We have a saying that is quite true: Either Jesus is Lord of all, or he is not Lord at all. You cannot profess to be his disciple without following him in all things and always.

If this mighty ruler from the tiny town of Bethlehem is not your ruler (for these or any of a number of other reasons), then what you need is to be reborn. Or to put it another way, Jesus needs to be born in you. Jesus was born in Bethlehem when he came to earth the first time. But now he also needs to be born in your heart, wherever you may live.

Do you recall that wonderful last stanza of Phillips Brooks lovely carol about Bethlehem? The early stanzas describe the little village on a quiet winter night, marvelling at the silent way 'the wondrous gift is given'.

They progress to the fact that it is in precisely that way, silently, that the gift must come to each of us. The one whose origins are of old must quietly become incarnate in our hearts.

Then comes the last stanza, which is a prayer.

O holy child of Bethlehem,
    Descend to us, we pray;
Cast out our sin, and enter in,
    Be born in us today.
We hear the Christmas angels
    The great glad tidings tell;
O come to us, abide with us,
Our Lord Emmanuel.

If you are a church-goer (or even if you are not), you have probably sung that carol many hundreds of times. But the next time you sing it, wouldn't it be wonderful if you could sing it honestly and with understanding? If you would like to, the way to do it is to invite Jesus into your heart now. You need to confess your sin, thank him for his great love and grace in dying for you, and promise to follow him from this time onward as your Lord.

If you do that, the angels who sang in the skies above Bethlehem at Christ's birth will burst into praise once again. For Jesus said that there is joy in heaven over even one sinner who repents of sin and turns to him.

PART TWO

THE ANNOUNCEMENT

4

CALL HIM 'JESUS'
(Matthew 1:18-25)

This is how the birth of Jesus came about: His mother Mary was pledged to be married to Joseph, but before they came together, she was found to be with child through the Holy Spirit. Because Joseph her husband was a righteous man and did not want to expose her to public disgrace, he had in mind to divorce her quietly.

But after he had considered this, an angel of the Lord appeared to him in a dream and said, 'Joseph son of David, do not be afraid to take Mary home as your wife, because what is conceived in her is from the Holy Spirit. She will give birth to a son, and you are to give him the name Jesus, because he will save his people from their sins.'

All this took place to fulfil what the Lord had said through the prophet: 'The virgin will be with child and will give birth to a son, and they will call him Immanuel' – which means, 'God with us.'

When Joseph woke up, he did what the angel of the Lord had commanded him and took Mary home as his wife. But he had no union with her until she gave birth to a son. And he gave him the name Jesus.

One of the things that has struck me in a new light as I have reread the Christmas story is the role the angels play in it. It has occurred to me that apart from the angels no one would have understood what the birth of the Lord Jesus Christ was about – not Joseph, not Mary, not the shepherds. Apart from the angels' message the incarnation would have remained a mystery to everyone.

The conception of Jesus would have puzzled Mary, of course. She would have wondered how she could have conceived without having known a man. Yet the significance of the incarnation would have been beyond her. Would she have guessed what was happening by being familiar with the Old Testament prophecies, like Isaiah's prophecy that 'the virgin will be with child and will give birth to a son' (Isa. 7:14)? At best Mary might have guessed that the child that was born of her might be the Messiah. But she could not have known that for sure.

Nor would Joseph have known. Joseph would only have thought that Mary had been unfaithful to him, which he did think for a time anyway.

And the shepherds would not have come to the manger in the little town of Bethlehem – if the angels had not given them their great message.

Moreover, it seems to me that apart from the truths the angels revealed to these people of the Christmas story, the real meaning of the birth of Jesus will undoubtedly pass us by also. The world will not allow us to miss the holiday. We will always have Christmas, and there will always be a great deal of Christmas sentiment, some happiness and much activity. But this is all there will be unless the angel appears with his message, which is a way of saying that we will only understand the meaning of the birth of Christ by a God-directed revelation.

The Appearance to Joseph
There are five appearances of an angel or angels in the Christmas story, plus another appearance a few years later to tell Joseph to return to Israel from Egypt, where he had gone to escape the wrath of King Herod.

They are: (1) the appearance of Gabriel to Zechariah to announce the birth of John the Baptist, (2) the appearance of Gabriel to Mary to announce the birth of Jesus, (3) the appearance of an unnamed angel to Joseph to explain the Virgin Birth and to name the child, (4) the appearance of first one angel and then a multitude of angels to the shepherds above the fields surrounding Bethlehem, and (5) an appearance to Joseph in a dream to tell him to take his family to Egypt because of Herod.

Chronologically the order is as I have given it. But in the order of the New Testament books the very first appearance is to Joseph.

Think of the spiritual condition of the Jewish people at this point in their history. There had been revelations from God in the past, through such great men of God as Isaiah, Jeremiah, Ezekiel, Daniel and the so-called minor prophets, but for over four hundred years the prophetic voice had been silent. Malachi, who had lived in the fifth century before Christ, was the last of the prophets. The Old Testament ends with his book. Since his day no one had been raised up to declare a sure word from God. Had God forgotten his people? Had the Lord cast them off? We turn to the New Testament, and there in the very first chapter we find the appearance of the angel to him who was to be the adoptive father of Mary's divine child.

'Jehovah is Salvation'
The appearance of the angel to Joseph was to explain why and how Mary was expecting a child so that he would marry her and protect her rather than break the

engagement quietly. But the message also recognised Joseph's authority and responsibility to name Mary's child. So Joseph was told, 'Do not be afraid to take Mary home as your wife, because what is conceived in her is from the Holy Spirit. She will give birth to a son, and you are to give him the name Jesus, because he will save his people from their sins' (vv. 20, 21). This name had also been given to Mary when the angel appeared to her earlier (cf. Luke 1:31).

What a name this was!

Jesus is the Greek form of the Hebrew name Jehoshua, Jeshua or Joshua, and it means literally 'Jehovah is Salvation'. So the message to Joseph centred primarily on the great work Jesus was to do. Jesus was to be the agent of God's salvation, and his work was to 'save his people from their sins,' as the angel explained clearly.

It is unfortunate that the words 'Saviour' and 'salvation' have been so watered down in our day, because to many people they convey only a fraction of what the terms actually imply. They have been watered down even by Christian theologians.

One person who has been responsible for this is Paul Tillich, the German-born American theologian, now deceased. Tillich developed his understanding of salvation from the meaning of the Latin word *salvus*, from which the English word comes. *Salvus* means 'healthy' or 'whole'. So Tillich, who popularised this approach in his three-volume Systematic Theology, taught that salvation should be understood as 'every act of healing ... the healing of sickness, of demonic possession, and of servitude to sin and to the ultimate power of death'.[1] It means 'reuniting that which is estranged, giving a centre to what is split, overcoming the split between God and man, man and his world, man and

---

[1] Paul Tillich, *Systematic Theology*, (Chicago: University of Chicago Press, 1951), vol. 1, p.146.

himself.'[2] Most people do not read Paul Tillich, of course. His writings are difficult even for theologians. But this unfortunate approach has found its way into an avalanche of books on pastoral counselling, Christian psychiatry, missions, Christian social work and the cure of souls.

The difficulty with it is not that salvation is unrelated to such things as counselling and social work. In fact, the opposite is the case. There are many references in the Bible to deliverance from disease, poverty, captivity or physical death. The difficulty lies in the fact that today, if only because of the impressive achievements of medical science, no distinction is made between the salvation God alone can bring and the kinds of salvation we are capable of achieving for ourselves. What, for instance, is the difference between the wholeness experienced by a member of a church in the course of a counselling session with his or her minister, in which the person comes to genuine faith in Christ, and the wholeness gained by an atheist as the result of a similar session with a reputable but non-Christian psychiatrist?

Unless our way of talking about salvation makes distinctions here, our interpretations fall woefully short of what the angel was talking about when he said that Jesus would 'save his people from their sins'.

Another example of the way modern churchmen have reduced the biblical view of salvation to mere human dimensions is the increasing emphasis placed on social aspects of the gospel, as opposed to evangelism as traditionally understood. Beyond any doubt, the gospel has social implications. Wherever the gospel has gone schools, orphanages, hospitals and other care facilities have followed. Moreover, Christians are to be active in all such efforts to achieve social justice, improve the lives of

---

[2] Paul Tillich, *Systematic Theology*, (Chicago: University of Chicago Press, 1957), vol. 2, p.166.

the poor and minister to people who are needy. But that is not what the Bible is talking about when it speaks of salvation or what the angel had in mind when he gave the name Jesus to Joseph for his naming of the child.

When the Bible talks about salvation, primarily it is talking about salvation from sin – from its penalty and from its power. And that is what Jesus came to achieve for us. If we could save ourselves, which many of the liberal understandings of salvation suggest, there would have been no need for Jesus to have been born. There would have been no need for his life, his death on the cross or his resurrection. But we cannot save ourselves, not from sin at all and not very much even from the social problems sin has created.

Jesus had to come. His birth was necessary. For that reason, the promise of the angel, embodied in the name Jesus, is the greatest message of the entire Christmas story and, in fact, of all time.

'You are to give him the name Jesus, because he will save his people from their sins.' Jesus fulfilled that promise when he died on the cross for our sin and rose again for our justification.

'God With Us'

But there is more in the name Jesus even than this. Earlier, when I was explaining the literal meaning of the name, I said that Jesus was the agent of God's salvation. That is true, but it is not the whole truth. The name also means that Jesus is the Saviour-God himself.

This is undoubtedly why Matthew followed up on his report of the angel's words to Joseph by referring to Isaiah's prophecy of the Virgin Birth and to the name Immanuel, which was given at that time: 'All this took place to fulfil what the Lord had said through the prophet: "The virgin will be with child and will give birth to a son, and they

will call him Immanuel" – which means, "God with us"'
(vv. 22, 23).

In its ancient context this prophetic sign may have
concerned only a normal birth of a son to a young woman,
since the Hebrew word *almah* can mean 'a young woman
of marriageable age,' as well as 'virgin'. But whatever the
original meaning may have been, there is no question of
the way in which Matthew refers it to Jesus. Matthew says
that the prophecy was of the virgin conception, teaching
that by it the eternal Son of God himself became a man to
accomplish our salvation.

This is an astonishing teaching, of course. In the Old
Testament it is often said that God was *for* his people. That
is, he is the one who guided their destinies and intervened in
history to effect some great deliverance or victory for them.
God's advocacy was a great thing. But it is surely an even
greater thing that, by means of the incarnation, God who
before was only *for* his people, now is *with* them. Now he has
become as we are. He has taken our nature to himself.

This is what captured the imagination of Charles
Wesley when he composed the second stanza of his great
Christmas hymn: *Hark! The Herald Angels Sing*. Wesley
must have had these passages in mind, for his stanza moves
from Jesus' heavenly pre-existence to his incarnation, and
then ends with the powerful name 'Immanuel'.

> Christ, by highest heaven adored,
> Christ, the everlasting Lord!
> Late in time behold him come,
> Offspring of the virgin's womb.
> Veiled in flesh the Godhead see;
> Hail the incarnate deity,
> Pleased as man with men to dwell,
> Jesus, our Emmanuel.
> Hark! the herald angels sing,
> 'Glory to the newborn King.'

It is as the incarnate Son of God that Jesus achieved our salvation, and it is as the eternal God-man that he now represents us and intercedes for us before the Father.

Always With Us

The continuing presence of Jesus with us is worth thinking about in some detail. For if it is true that the eternal Son of God is with us through the incarnation and continues to be with us, then all the experiences of the believer's life are or should be transformed. All of them! Nothing should be the same for us since the incarnation.

(1) *In joy and in sorrow*

If God is for us and with us in Christ, then he is with us in all our joys and in all our sorrows. Think back over your life and ask yourself what were the very best times you have experienced. Were they the days of your childhood? The days when you first left home and started out to earn a living on your own? The days of your courtship? Your marriage? Perhaps your best days are right now, in what you are doing or achieving in your work or in the Lord's service.

Whatever the case, haven't those days been enhanced by the presence of the Lord Jesus Christ? Wouldn't they have been entirely different without him? One of the old collects of the church has these words: 'Almighty and ever-blessed God, whose presence is the happiness of every condition and whose favour hallows every relation....' That is it exactly. Jesus being with us makes all our joys better.

And he helps in the sorrows too. For most of us life contains many good things, but it also has its share of sorrows. We lose those we have loved. We get sick. Sometimes we lose our jobs or fortunes. Happily, Jesus is with us in these times too, and he helps us because he understands us. After all, he too was 'a man of sorrows, and familiar with suffering' (Isa. 53:3). He too was hungry. He too was misunderstood. Eventually he was betrayed and crucified. Many Christians testify that their times of sweetest fellowship with Jesus have been when they have been forsaken by someone else or have been forced to undergo some suffering.

(2) *In temptation*
Jesus is also 'God with us' when we are tempted. It is good he is, because temptations do come. We are not exempt from them just because we are Christians. In fact, in one sense, temptations will be even worse, because the evil one will attack us as he did not attack when we were still living in his kingdom. But although the struggle to obey the Lord Jesus Christ and do right may be hard at times and we may sometimes even think we would like to abandon our Christian profession and live like the devil's own people, Jesus will be with us even then and will not let us run freely with the wicked. He will be with us and will keep working in us until we achieve the victory. And that leads to the next point.

(3) *In spiritual warfare against Satan*
Jesus is with us in our spiritual warfare. Paul wrote to the Ephesians, 'Our struggle is not against flesh and blood, but against the rulers, against the authorities, against the powers of this dark world and against the spiritual forces of evil in the heavenly realms' (Eph. 6:12). That is formidable opposition. If we were able to see these spiritual forces or were confronted by them openly, we would all no doubt be utterly terrified. A vision of Satan would be overwhelming for us. Left to ourselves we would be overcome. But we are not left to ourselves. That is the point. God is with us. Jesus is with us. 'Those

who are with us are more than those who are with them' (2 Kings 6:16).

In Ephesians 6 Paul writes that God has provided armour and weapons for our warfare: a 'belt of truth' buckled around our waist (v. 14), a 'breastplate of righteousness' (v. 14), our 'feet fitted with the readiness that comes from the gospel of peace' (v. 15), 'the shield of faith' (v. 16), a 'helmet of salvation' (v. 17) and 'the sword of the Spirit, which is the word of God' (v. 17). But each of these actually stands for Jesus himself. A belt of truth? Jesus is the truth (John 14:6). A breastplate of righteousness? Jesus is our righteousness (1 Cor. 1:30). The gospel of peace? Jesus is himself the very message of the gospel, the good news. Faith? Faith is Christ's gift (Eph. 2:8, 9). The helmet of salvation? Jesus means 'Jehovah is Salvation,' as we saw earlier. The sword of the Spirit, which is the Word of God? Jesus is the Logos, the Word himself (John 1:1, 14). It is because Jesus is 'God with us' that we have these spiritual weapons and can stand victorious against the forces of evil in this age.

(4) *To the very end*
Moreover, this is going to be true for us until the very end, that is, until Jesus returns for us or when we die and go to be with him.

At the very end of the Great Commission, in the words that complete Matthew's Gospel, there is a sentence that takes us back to the name Immanuel, which we found at the beginning. Jesus has told his disciples that all authority in heaven and on earth has been given to him and has instructed them to go into all the world and there make disciples of all nations. He has told them how this is to be done. They are to baptise in the name of the Father and of the Son and of the Holy Spirit, and they are to teach obedience to everything he has commanded. Then he concludes, 'And surely I am with you always, to the very end of the age' (Matt. 28:20).

With you? With us?

Yes, and to the very end of this age!

At the beginning of the gospel Jesus is 'God with us' by the incarnation. Here at the end he is still 'God with us'. He is with us in our joys and sorrows, in our testings and trials, in our spiritual battles. Even in the moment of our deaths. Always with us, until the age ends and the entire church of God is ushered into the eternal bliss of heaven. And even then he will be with us. For on the eve of his crucifixion he told his disciples, 'I am going ... to prepare a place for you. And if I go and prepare a place for you, I will come back and take you to be with me that you also may be where I am' (John 14:2-3).

Name of All Names

There are many names for Jesus. The Bible is full of them. He is the First and the Last, the Beginning and the End, the Alpha and the Omega, the Ancient of Days. He is King of Kings and Lord of Lords. He is the Anointed One, the Messiah. He is the Prophet and the Priest. He is the Saviour, the Only Wise God our Saviour. He is our Wonderful Counsellor, the Mighty God, the Everlasting Father, the Prince of Peace. He is the Almighty. He is the Lord. He is the Door of the Sheep, the Good Shepherd, the Great Shepherd, the Chief Shepherd, the Shepherd and Bishop of our souls. He is the Lamb, the Lamb Without Spot or Blemish, the Lamb Slain from before the Foundation of the World. He is the Logos, the Light, the Light of the World, the Light of Life, the Tree of Life, the Word of Life, the Bread that Came down from Heaven, the Spring which, if a person drink of it, he will never thirst again. He is the Way, the Truth and the Life. He is the Resurrection, the Resurrection and the Life. He is our

Rock, our Bridegroom, our Beloved. He is our Redeemer. He is the One who is Altogether Lovely. He is the Head over all things which is his body, the church. He is God with Us, Immanuel.

But above all, he is Jesus. Jesus.

We love him for that name, because his name means 'Jehovah is Salvation' and he came to save his people from their sins.

5

Three Miracles of Christmas

(Luke 1:26-38)

In the sixth month, God sent the angel Gabriel to Nazareth, a town in Galilee, to a virgin pledged to be married to a man named Joseph, a descendant of David. The virgin's name was Mary. The angel went to her and said, 'Greetings, you who are highly favoured! The Lord is with you.'

Mary was greatly troubled at his words and wondered what kind of greeting this might be. But the angel said to her, 'Do not be afraid, Mary, you have found favour with God. You will be with child and give birth to a son, and you are to give him the name Jesus. He will be great and will be called the Son of the Most High. The Lord God will give him the throne of his father David, and he will reign over the house of Jacob for ever; his kingdom will never end.'

'How will this be,' Mary asked the angel, 'since I am a virgin?'

The angel answered, 'The Holy Spirit will come upon you, and the power of the Most High will overshadow you. So the holy one to be born will be called the Son of God. Even Elizabeth your relative is going to have a child in her old age, and she who was said to be barren is in her sixth month. For nothing is impossible with God.'

'I am the Lord's servant,' Mary answered. 'May it be to me as you have said.' Then the angel left her.

There is something about Christmas that is wonderful – in spite of the frantic pace of the days leading up to Christmas, the anxious flurry of pre-Christmas buying and the undisguised commercialism and materialism that is so much a part of Christmas in the west.

I suppose it is the sheer magnitude of the event itself, the grandeur of what Christmas means: the birth of the Saviour.

And the miracles! We often say that the birth of any baby is a miracle, meaning that life is a miracle. And it is. We cannot create life. Life is God's gift. But in the case of Christmas, the miracles are so much bigger even than that. In my judgment the miracles of Christmas are greater even than the miracles Jesus did in his lifetime – healing the lepers, giving sight to the blind and strength to the lame, raising the dead to life – greater even than the climactic resurrection of Jesus himself on the third day following his crucifixion. And there is something of the wonder of these miracles in our observances of Christmas even for modern people, like ourselves, who have such difficulty with the miraculous.

The miracles are there from the very beginning from the moment in which the angel Gabriel announced the conception and birth of Jesus to the humble virgin of Nazareth, whose name was Mary.

Martin Luther and Saint Bernard
Martin Luther was such a vigorous and original person that I have often turned to him to see what he had to say about some well-known text, like the verses in which

Gabriel announces the birth of Jesus to Mary. When I did that for these verses I discovered that Luther himself sometimes turned to other people and that, in this case, he turned to Saint Bernard, the godly French monk who lived in the twelfth century.

Luther quotes Bernard as saying that there are three miracles in this story: (1) 'that God and man should be joined in this child,' (2) 'that a mother should remain a virgin,' and (3) 'that Mary should have such faith as to believe that this mystery would be accomplished in her'. He adds perceptively that 'the last is not the least of the three'. [1]

I find this to be a fresh way to look at the announcement of the birth of Christ and so take it as a guide for this study.

That God Should Become Man

The announcement that Jesus should be born to Mary has several parts, all of them important: that Jesus would be 'great'; that he would be 'the Son of the Most High'; that he would be 'holy,' that is, without sin; and that he would 'reign over the house of Jacob' on the throne of David for ever. But of these various parts of the announcement the greatest, without any doubt, is that the one to be born should be the Son of God. It is the greatest part of the announcement because it means that by the incarnation and birth God would himself become man.

This is an amazing miracle, of course. It is contrary to anything we might expect and beyond anything we can fully understand. God created all things. A human being is part of that creation. How, we might ask, can it be possible for God to become part of that which he created? The answer defies philosophical explanation.

---

[1] Martin Luther, *The Martin Luther Christmas Book*, trans. and arranged by Roland H. Bainton (Philadelphia: Fortress Press, 1948), pp. 22, 23.

I am sure you know how great a problem this was for the citizens of the ancient world. It was a problem for the Jew, because the Jew regarded God as being so high above his creation that the doctrine of the incarnation debased him and was therefore thought to be blasphemous. Besides, the incarnation seemed to teach that there were two gods, one in heaven and one on earth in the form of the alleged Messiah, and that offended Jewish monotheism.

The incarnation was also a problem for the Gentile because, in spite of the popular myths about gods consorting with humans, the ancients believed in an unbridgeable gulf between spirit, which is what God is, and flesh, which is at least part of what it means to be a human being. Spirit is not flesh, nor could it become flesh, according to ancient thinking. Therefore, for those whose minds were formed by such categories of thought any literal incarnation of God was judged to be impossible.

These views were so strong in the ancient world that even in Christian circles some early heresies tried to explain the incarnation by saying that the spirit of Christ came on the man Jesus, rather loosely, at the time of his baptism and left him just before his crucifixion.

But it is not only the ancient world that had trouble with the miracle of the incarnation. Our modern world has trouble with it too, largely because we disbelieve in nearly everything, especially the miraculous. Even some alleged Christians disbelieve it.

A few years ago a British scholar named John Hick edited a book with the title *The Myth of God Incarnate*, which attempted to dismiss the incarnation as simple but ignorant and profoundly-mistaken mythology. The thesis of the book was, not surprisingly, that the incarnation was a myth. Today few unregenerate people do literally affirm the incarnation of God. The only surprising thing about this book was that Hick and those who contributed to it thought they could maintain Christianity without the incarnation and that they could continue to call themselves Christians while rejecting it.

Their underlying premise was that Christianity needs constantly to adapt itself into 'something which can be believed,' and that in today's world it has to become an incarnationless religion. [2]

Well, 'that God and man should be joined in this child' is certainly a miracle, as Luther said. The acceptance of miracles requires faith. But that does not mean that the miracle itself is unreasonable or meaningless.

That God should become a man may seem strange to some forms of human philosophy, but it is not beyond the ability of God to accomplish. God can do anything he chooses consistent with his own nature. And as far as the reason for the incarnation is concerned, the remainder of the New Testament makes clear that it was necessary for Jesus to become man in order to die for us and thereby achieve our salvation. God must punish sin. We are sinners. The punishment for sin is death (Rom. 6:23). Therefore we must die for our sin – unless another, who is innocent of all wrong himself and who is of sufficient value in God's eyes to make atonement for others, should bear the punishment due to us in our place. That is exactly what Jesus has done, of course. It is what the incarnation is about.

That God should join with man in this child is the first great miracle of Christmas.

The Virgin Birth
The second miracle of Christmas announced to Mary by the angel Gabriel is the Virgin Birth. Strangely, this miracle

---

[2] John Hick, editor, and others *The Myth of God Incarnate* (Philadelphia: The Westminster Press, 1977), p. ix. The authors got the idea of constant adaptation from T. S. Eliot.

was not a problem for the ancients. At least no strong opposition to its being possible has been recorded. It is only in recent times, in the earlier decades of this century, that the Virgin Birth has been discounted. It was attacked by the unbelieving liberal element in Christianity.

God always has his champions, of course. And in this case his champion was a New Testament scholar by the name of J. Gresham Machen. Machen examined the matter as only a scholar of his outstanding stature could. He showed that the idea of the Virgin Birth was not something added to Christianity at some later time through error, deceit or superstition but that it was present in Christianity from the earliest possible moment, is preserved in the earliest portions of the New Testament sources, and is probably to be traced to the earliest possible witness to the Virgin Birth, namely, Mary herself. So exhaustive and brilliant was Machen's book that no one, not even the most articulate or militant of the liberal scholars, answered it.[3] They could not, because the doctrine is true and Machen's points were unassailable.

True, we do not know how God could cause a virgin to conceive and so bear his Son. The conception is clearly a miracle. But that God did so is no less clearly a fact of human history.

Is the fact important?

How could it not be? The Virgin Birth is important because it proves that Jesus Christ is the only begotten Son of God. He has a divine as well as a fully human nature. It is important because it fixes the moment of the incarnation at the conception of Jesus rather than at some later point as some liberal theologies would have it. It enforces the utter sinlessness of the Saviour. Jesus needed to be sinless if he were to accomplish the mission for which the Father

---

[3] J Gresham Machen, *The Virgin Birth of Christ* (London: James Clarke & Co, 1958).

sent him into the world. Only the Holy One of God could make an acceptable atonement for our sin.

Belief in Gabriel's Message

It is hard to think of Christmas without thinking of the two great miracles I have mentioned, the incarnation and the Virgin Birth, and yet the third of these three miracles is the greatest of all, namely, that Mary should believe the angel's message. Luther puts it nicely: 'The Virgin Birth is a mere trifle for God; that God should become man is a greater miracle; but most amazing of all is it that this maiden should credit [that is, believe] the announcement.'[4]

The great Baptist preacher Charles Haddon Spurgeon has a sermon on this passage in which he compares the question of Mary in verse 34 ('How will this be since I am a virgin?') with Zechariah's similar question in verse 18 ('How can I be sure of this?'). He calls it *A Distinction with a Difference*. What he means by this title is that, although the words of the two figures are very much alike, there is nevertheless an enormous and important difference between their meanings and the ways they were asked.

Zechariah's question expressed his disbelief. The angel had appeared to him to announce the conception and birth of John the Baptist, just as he later appeared to Mary to announce the birth of Jesus. However, in Zechariah's case there was no miracle of God becoming man; John was a mere human being, though a great one. There was no Virgin Birth; John's was a natural conception. The only problem for Zechariah was that his wife Elizabeth was up in years and was therefore probably past the age of having children. Zechariah was God's priest. He knew the Old Testament. He must have been aware of the story in

---

[4] Martin Luther, *The Martin Luther Christmas Book*, p. 23.

which Abraham was given a son when he was past the age of engendering one and when Sarah was past the age of conceiving. Yet in spite of this and in spite of the fact that an angel actually appeared to him to make the announcement of John's birth, Zechariah did not believe the angel's message. Therefore he was struck dumb until after the birth of John the Baptist nine months later. His inability to speak was to be a sign to him. The angel said, 'You will be silent and not able to speak until the day this happens, because you did not believe my words, which will come true at their proper time' (v. 20).

How different in the case of Mary! On the surface Mary seems to say nearly the same thing. 'How will this be,' she asks, 'since I am a virgin?' But there is all the difference in the world between what Zechariah said and the way Mary asks her question. Mary did not say, 'How can I be sure of this?' She was sure of it. God had spoken through his angel. Mary believed what God said. Her question had to do rather with how this great miracle was to happen. Her question was an example of what the later medieval theologian Anselm of Canterbury was to call *fides quarens intellectum* ('Faith in search of understanding').

And this is precisely what God gave her, understanding. For the angel went on to explain what should happen, as thoroughly as it is possible to explain such a miracle. The angel said, 'The Holy Spirit will come upon you, and the power of the Most High will overshadow you' (v. 35).

Moreover, although Mary did not ask for a sign as Zechariah did, God nevertheless gave her one, for the angel continued his announcement by saying, 'Even Elizabeth your relative is going to have a child in her old age, and she who was said to be barren is in her sixth month. For nothing is impossible with God' (vv. 36, 37). That was important to Mary, as we know. Mary went to stay with her cousin Elizabeth until near the time of her delivery.

There are two great examples for us here. For, as Spurgeon observed, we should imitate Mary both in her implicit faith in the promises of God and in her inquiry. God honours faith and delights to teach the one who has it. He loves to instruct the one who believes him implicitly.[5]

'Be Born in Us Today'
At this point I have spoken of three great miracles of Christmas: that God should become man, that he should do so by means of a Virgin Birth, and that Mary should have believed the angel's announcement. But now I want to say that the last of these miracles needs to have its counterpart in us. We too need to believe the good news concerning this child, that he is the Saviour sent by the Father to deliver us from sin, and we need to commit ourselves to him in wholehearted trust and obedience.

Moreover, I want to say also that if we do – and believing God requires no less a miracle in us than in the case of Mary – then there is a sense in which the other two miracles happen also: (1) God is born in us, and (2) this is a Virgin Birth in the sense that it is accomplished by God alone, apart from any human contribution.

I think the Apostle Peter must have been thinking along these lines when he wrote of Christians, 'You have been born again, not of perishable seed, but of imperishable, through the living and enduring word of God' (1 Pet. 1:23). That means we do not become Christians by anything we or any other human being does or can do but by the miracle of a divine birth. And if we ask, as Mary did, 'How can this be since I am a sinner?' that is, 'since there is no uncontaminated good in me,' the answer is: 'The Holy Spirit will come upon you, and the power of the Most High will overshadow you.'

---

[5] Charles Haddon Spurgeon, 'A Distinction with a Difference' in *Metropolitan Tabernacle Pulpit*, vol. 24 (Pasadena, Texas: Pilgrim Publications, 1972), pp. 169-180. Original edition 1878.

Jesus taught this truth to Nicodemus when he told that teacher in Israel, 'Unless a man is born of water and the Spirit, he cannot enter the kingdom of God' (John 3:5).

Martin Luther does not say it quite this way, but he was thinking along these same lines when he wrote of Mary, 'She held fast to the word of the angel because she had become a new creature. [That is, she had been born again.] Even so must we be transformed and renewed in heart from day to day. Otherwise Christ is born in vain. [For] this is the word of the prophet: "*Unto us* a child is born, *unto us* a son is given" (Isa. 9:6).'

He adds, 'This is for us the hardest point, not so much to believe that [Jesus] is the Son of the Virgin and God himself, as to believe that this Son of God is ours.'[6]

I do not understand miracles. I do not think anyone does, otherwise the miracles would not be miracles by definition. But I believe in miracles, and I know that there would be no Christianity – no Christmas, no Saviour, no hope, no gospel, no salvation at all – unless these miracles truly happened. Moreover, I know that the miracles need to continue in us if Christianity is to continue as true Christianity and sinners are to be saved.

What needs to happen?

What needs to happen is what we sing about in that simple little carol written by Phillips Brooks after a visit to the Holy Land in 1866: *O Little Town of Bethlehem*. The carol describes the sleeping town in stanza one, the miraculous birth in stanza two, the quiet of the moment in stanza three. Then comes stanza four, the most important of all.

O holy child of Bethlehem,
   Descend to us, we pray;
Cast out our sin, and enter in,
   Be born in us today.

---

[6] Martin Luther, *The Martin Luther Christmas Book*, p. 23

We hear the Christmas angels
   The great glad tidings tell:
O come to us, abide with us,
   Our Lord Emmanuel.

The hymn begins with Christmas in Bethlehem, but it ends with Christmas in our hearts. And so it must be for each of us, if Christ is not to be 'born in vain' where we are concerned, to use Luther's terminology.

The mystical seventeenth century poet, Angelus Silesius, wrote:

Should Christ be born a thousand times anew,
Despair, O man, unless he's born in you. [7]

That is what Christmas is about, and it is what I urge on you this Christmas. Do not stop with the story of the birth of Christ itself. Do not stop even with the miracles of that first Christmas, great as they are. Press on in the matter until you can say, as Christians have always said, 'The miracles of Christmas have happened in my heart. I have been born again, and therefore I now place my entire trust for this life and for eternity in him who came to earth on that long-ago day and far-away land to be my Saviour.'

Miracles happen quietly. I do not expect any loud noise if that greatest of all miracles takes place in your heart. But I know that if it is happening or has happened, the angels are singing about it – if not where you can hear them, at least in heaven. Jesus himself said that there is more joy in heaven over one sinner who repents and believes the good news than over ninety-nine righteous persons who do not think they need it.

---

[7] From Frank Colquhoun, *Hymns That Live: Their Meaning and Message* (Downers Grove, Ill.: InterVarsity Press, 1980), p. 59.

6

Isn't it Absurd?

(Luke 1:34)

'How will this be,' Mary asked the angel, 'since I am a virgin?'

Most people are familiar with the story in which Gabriel is sent to Nazareth to announce the future birth of Jesus to the virgin Mary. I want to ask a question of that announcement, indeed of the Christmas story and even of Christianity as a whole. My question is: Isn't it absurd?

Preachers are not supposed to ask this kind of question. They are not even to suggest that it might be reasonable to ask it. But, naturally, the question is in people's minds anyway, and it was even in Mary's mind, although she did not ask it in an unbelieving way. When the angel appeared to her to say that she would conceive and give birth to a son and that the conception of her child would be without a male agent, that the baby would have no human father, Mary said, 'How will this be since I am a virgin?'

There are different ways of asking God questions. You can ask, 'How can this be?' and be quite unbelieving. That was the case with Zechariah in the earlier part of the chapter. God told him that John the Baptist would be born of himself and his wife Elizabeth when they were both very old, and Zechariah asked, 'How can I be sure of this?' (Luke 1:18). It was an unbelieving question, and he was judged for it, though mildly. Zechariah was unable to speak until the child was born and then named according to the angel's instructions.

A person can also ask, 'How?' in a believing way, which is what Mary did. And yet, the questions deal with the same thing. As long as we are thinking on the basis of known physical laws, what God was promising Mary was impossible. And to say that it is impossible is really only another way of saying, 'It's absurd.'

And, of course, the virgin birth is not the only absurd thing about the story, if you approach it on the basis of known laws. In some ways the entire life and work of Jesus is absurd.

An Impossible Birth

Think of the birth, first of all, even apart from the miracle involved in the conception of a child by a virgin. It was not the birth of a normal human child. There is nothing absurd about a normal human birth. What makes this birth absurd from a mere human point of view is that it is also said to be the birth of God, that is, the birth of one who was both man and God, as the great creeds of the church describe him.

How can that be?

Isn't it absurd to think that the infinite, exalted, distant, holy God of the universe – a God we cannot even see – should make himself man, a man who could not only be seen, handled and touched, but also, as we very well know, could be crucified?

The incarnation was absurd to the Greeks. The basic principle of Greek philosophy was the radical distinction between what is spiritual and what is physical, usually expressed as the distinction between spirit and body or mind and matter. According to Greek thought, the two could never be mingled. To the Greek mind it was the height of absurdity to think that God, who is the basis for all reality and is non-material, could take on human flesh. The result was that when the church spread from Jerusalem into areas of the world dominated by Greek thought, heresies began to emerge which taught that God was not really incarnate in Jesus Christ but rather that Jesus was only a man and that God simply came upon him in a certain way – possessed him, as it were – and then left him before the crucifixion, since God could not die either according to this thinking.

But we can ask the identical question, though for different reasons. Isn't it absurd to think that God himself, the very God of all creation, should become a man?

And isn't it absurd that this God-man, Jesus, should be born in a stable? If this child was really God, as the Bible claims, we would expect him to have had the most honoured, most exalted birth of all. It is true that angels appeared, singing in the night sky, but they were heard only by shepherds, so far as we know. Isn't the incarnation the sort of thing that should have been published everywhere? Shouldn't the birth of Jesus have caused angels to go throughout every city, town and hamlet on the face of the earth, proclaiming, 'Jesus, the Son of God, has been born in Bethlehem of Judea. Come and worship him.' In past periods of history, when a son was born to a king heralds were sent throughout the realm to proclaim the heir's arrival. Yet here, in the case of the birth of the very Son of God, almost nothing is said. It just happens – in a far-away land, in a small town, to a couple who had no worldly status and did not even have a place to stay that night, the inn being full.

Then there was the miraculous conception. Mary was disturbed by it, and others have been disturbed since. Isn't it absurd to think – even granting that it is possible for God to become man and that this should take place in a stable for some reason – isn't it absurd to think that this could happen by means of a virgin conception? How could a woman conceive without a male agent? We know enough biology to know that such a thing is impossible. To have a conception, you have to have male sperm and a female egg. Lacking either, you do not have life. So how can it be that this ovum in the womb of Mary suddenly began to grow, with no male involvement? That goes against all the laws of nature, as we know them.

An Impossible Life
Not only do we see absurdities in the origins of Jesus Christ. We see them in his life as well. For the first thirty years of his life he lived in complete obscurity. Then suddenly, at about the age of thirty, he appeared near the Jordan river, was baptised by his relative, John the Baptist, went into the Judean desert, where he was tempted by the devil and overcame him and, at that point, began a three-year ministry in which he travelled throughout the obscure land of Palestine. The farthest he ever got from it was to go north in the direction of Sidon or across on the Sea of Galilee to an area known as the Decapolis. He taught people about God. He did miracles. He walked upon the Sea of Galilee. He turned water into wine. He multiplied fish and loaves in order to feed great gatherings of people. He healed lepers. Eventually, so the story says, he raised the dead.

Then came his arrest and crucifixion. And we discover that this one who was able to do miracles in the lives of others – who was even able to perform resurrections

– was, as people said about him at the time, unable, so it would seem, to save himself.

Isn't that absurd?

Isn't it absurd that this divine Saviour, if he really was the Saviour, should die, and in that way? Indeed, if we grant the premise that he was the Son of God as well as being a man, isn't it absurd to think that God should die? For how can God die? Isn't God eternal? Yet that is what happened in some sense in the case of Jesus Christ, according to the story.

Finally, as if that isn't sufficiently absurd, the story of his death is followed by accounts of the resurrection.

Now if there is one thing we know for sure, it is that dead people do not rise again. There is some difference among people today as to how long the human race has been around. Some religious people tend to have a very short span for human existence. Bishop Usher fixed the year of creation at 4,004 BC. Today others who are equally conservative push it back perhaps 15 to 20,000 years. On the other hand, people who study ancient civilisations and ancient human remains, say that men and women have been around for millions of years. Yet in all those years, whether they are reckoned in the thousands or the millions, so far as we can document – except for the stories in the Bible – nobody has ever come back from the dead. 'Once dead always dead' is our experience.

Yet Jesus was raised from the dead.

Isn't it absurd to think that this man, having been crucified in the sight of all Jerusalem so that everybody knew he was dead – there was no doubt about that – and having been buried, should rise again from the dead three days later and then wander around for forty more days teaching his disciples before going back to heaven?

And even that is bizarre. Instead of returning to heaven in what we might think of as a noble, mystical or even exciting way, he simply rose up from the earth, floated skyward and then disappeared into the clouds, leaving his disciples behind foolishly staring into heaven.

Not Absurd At All

How do you respond to that? I want to respond to it by suggesting that the answer to the question 'Isn't it absurd?' depends entirely upon how you ask it. One way of asking the question is to say, Aren't the facts of the story absurd by human standards? If we ask the question that way, the story may be absurd, as we have seen. But we can also ask the question in another way. We can ask, Is what the story is about absurd? Is what it teaches absurd? If we ask the question that way, the answer, as I hope to show, is that it is not absurd at all.

The problem I raised first, the incarnation of the second person of the Godhead in Jesus Christ, is the matter which the great medieval theologian, Anselm of Canterbury, wrestled with and wrote about so brilliantly in his book *Cur Deus Homo?* The title asks a question. It means, 'Why the God-man?' or 'Why did God become man?' – the very question I have been asking. Anselm took up the challenge of this question, saying, 'All right, let's investigate the problem. Let's see if it's absurd.' And he answers, as you might expect, by saying it is anything but absurd. Rather than being an absurdity, the incarnation is actually the wisdom of Almighty God.

God created man to have fellowship with himself. But man fell into sin which separated him from the Almighty and brought him under judgment. Anselm reasoned that it was not right that man, having fallen into sin, should be left to perish. It was necessary that God, who created him in the first place knowing that he would fall, should intervene for his salvation. But, asked Anselm, how was that to be done? The sin of man is a sin against God. If man has sinned against God, man is the one who must make restitution. Man must make the wrong right. But man is a sinner; and the sin against God is so great, so infinite in its offensive nature, that no mere man can make it right. The only One in the universe who can possibly make it right is God. But here is the dilemma! Man must pay the debt, but he cannot. Only God can pay it, but God is not man. How can the problem be resolved?

Anselm resolved it, as the Bible itself does, by the incarnation. God had to become man so that God, who alone could pay the price of man's redemption, might be in the person of the one who had to pay it. It is true that God cannot die, not as God. But in the person of Jesus Christ that is exactly what God did.

You see, when we talk about the meaning of what happened, we are talking theology, and it has been the task of theologians through the centuries to explain these apparently 'absurd' things. They have shown that they are not at all absurd when approached in this manner.

The God of Miracles
There is a third way our questions can be asked, however – not the mere 'whatness' of the story (what happened) or the mere meaning of events like the incarnation (why did it happen?) but rather *how* did it happen? How did the impossible come to be? And isn't that absurd?

Here we are on a different footing. When we begin to talk about the chief points of Jesus' life and work we are talking about things that admittedly are supernatural. There have been tendencies in the history of the church to try to explain the miracles away, to say, 'If we only had a few more details or understood a little more biology or physics or chemistry, then we would be able to explain how some of these things were done.' Well, it may be that, as human knowledge increases, some of the things that we find in the Bible may be explained scientifically, though I doubt it. But when we talk about miracles, we are talking, not just about matter – not just about physical things and physical laws – but about God, who created matter and who therefore, by definition, is different from and greater than matter. Such a God can obviously do whatever he wants with what he has created.

We live in an age when people think materialistically, as if what we can see and measure and touch is all that is. But that is not the nature of things according to the Bible. If there is a Creator who made us and all we touch and see – and that is the most rational thing of all – then there is also a reality which we cannot see and which is greater and more important. In other words, there is a spiritual or supernatural realm. And if that is true and if that realm is ruled by a supernatural and omnipotent God, then although it may be impossible for us to say how any particular miracle recorded in the Bible actually happened, it is nevertheless not irrational for us to believe that it did happen. God, the supernatural God, can do anything.

We should be led to acknowledge this even from the things we actually can see and know. Some years ago, a British writer by the name of John Ruskin wrote a parable called *An Ounce of Slime*. He imagined himself visiting a mill town where he sees a sewer near the mill pouring out what we would call slime. It is foul-smelling, ugly, of no value whatever. 'What is that slime composed of?' Ruskin asked.

He began to answer. 'Slime is a mixture of clay, sand, soot and water. Now,' said Ruskin, 'let's see what we can do with those substances. Let's take each of them and imagine each one of them worked upon so that it achieves its highest potential and greatest value.'

What happens when you take clay and purify it, as is often the case in nature? If you take the impurities out of the clay, you have white earth which, when it is formed by a skilled craftsman, can be turned into valuable porcelain – porcelain so valuable that it can sit upon a king's table. If you process it even further, in ways that we are unable to do but which nature itself knows – that is, within the earth, under pressure – the clay becomes clear and hard, gathers up the rays of the sun and becomes a jewel. The clay becomes a sapphire.

Take the sand and work upon it in the same manner. Under pressure the sand will also become hard and clear. It will reflect a variety of the sun's rays, reds and blues and greens. It becomes an opal.

Take the soot. Soot is carbon. What happens when you purify carbon, when you deal with it under pressure? It becomes the hardest substance known. It becomes absolutely clear. It becomes a diamond.

And the water? The water, which is so muddied by impurities that we think it is hardly fit for anything, purifies itself. Water evaporates, goes up into the sky, condenses and falls again as rain. In cold seasons of the year, it falls as snowflakes, some of the most beautiful things in nature, and every flake is different.

Here you have from this ounce of slime: a sapphire, an opal, a diamond and a snowflake. So it should not surprise us that, if God is able to create a world in which wonders like these can take place, God, who is above and greater than nature, can certainly do what we consider supernatural.

As a matter of fact, what is more reasonable than that God should not only be able to but actually *do* it in order to unfold the full potential and destiny of his creatures? We are physical creatures, of course, but we are more than physical. We have bodies, but we also have spirits and souls. So we need a Saviour who is not just a Saviour of the body – one who can save us from mere physical death – but also a Saviour of our spirits. We need one who is able to turn us from being the increasingly hard, bitter, arrogant, selfish people we are and make us like himself.

This is what God does. God takes the slime of our moral and spiritual lives and turns it into jewels which are able to sparkle before him for ever.

Love Has Its Reasons

I have tried to answer the question 'Isn't it absurd?' in several ways, dealing with what the story tells and with how it may have happened. I have tried to show that although there are elements to it that we certainly fail to understand, there is nevertheless nothing absurd about it. As a matter of fact, it is the most reasonable story in the universe.

But there is a final way in which we can answer the question – not asking what or how, but asking *why*? And I want to confess that if that is the question that we are asking – if we are asking why God should have done this – then I have no answer. Why God should have saved us is, humanly speaking, inexplicable.

God is the holy God. God made us in his image, to have fellowship with him. We by our own wills – not by the influence of the devil or the fault of God – we ourselves have made a muddle of our lives. More than that, we have done it in arrogant, wilful rebellion against God. We have turned our faces from him. We have shaken our fists in God's face. We have tried to build a world that is immune from God's good influence. We do not even want to hear the name of God acknowledged publicly. Why should God come to earth to save a race like that?

Why should God, the infinite God of the universe, take to himself the form of a helpless baby in the womb of a mother, be born in the pain of childbirth, be laid in a stable, grow up, be nailed to a cross and die an ignominious death? Why should God do that for us? Isn't that absurd?

There is an answer, of course. It may be an absurd answer, but it is still an answer. The answer is that God did it because he loved us.

Do you ever think of love being absurd? It often is, you know. Love has its reasons, and they do not always conform to human logic. You say, 'Why does Bill love Jane? I can't understand what he sees in her.' Well, it may be a strange relationship. But love has reasons which are known only to love.

God, why did you love us? Why did you send Jesus to be our Saviour?

How is God going to answer that question in terms that we can understand? Can God give us reasons? Can God explain his love to us? I don't think he can. God simply says, 'I did it because I love you.' And if we say to God, 'But why did you love us?' God answers, 'It is because I loved you.'

Moses explained that to Israel on one occasion. He was discussing the matter of election, the fact that God had elected Israel out of all the nations of the earth. And the question was asked, Why has God done this? It is a profound question, but Moses does not give an analytical answer. The text says simply, 'The Lord did not set his affection on you and choose you because you were more numerous than other peoples, for you were the fewest of all peoples. But it was because the Lord loved you and kept the oath he swore to your forefathers' (Deut. 7:7, 8). God loved them because he loved them. That is all.

My closing point is this, and it is a practical one. It says in 1 John 4:19, 'We love because he first loved us.' What that means is that if we have understood the Christmas story, we have understood at the most profound level – a level beyond which understanding cannot go – that God has done this because he loves us. And then, because he has loved us – and loved us in this way – we must love others also. Some of the older versions wrongly add the word 'him', saying, 'We love *him* because he first loved us.' And, of course, that is true. We do love him. But the text actually says, 'We love ....' We start by loving God, but we also love one another, even the unlovely, apart from 'reason', loving them as God has loved us.

Isn't that absurd?

Yes it is, if you are thinking about it as the world measures things. But that is Christianity, and it is that absurd but wonderful reality that is able to transform our wicked world.

7

THE IMPOSSIBLE POSSIBLE
FOR GOD

(Luke 1:37)

'Nothing is impossible with God.'

Six months after the angel Gabriel had appeared to Zechariah to announce the birth of John the Baptist, Gabriel also appeared to the Virgin Mary in Nazareth to announce the conception of Jesus Christ. The account is an engaging story, as Luke relates it to us: the humble maiden kneeling before the kind, bright angel; Gabriel unburdening himself of the message for which the faithful had been waiting for many long centuries; Mary's puzzled question ('How will this be?'); and the messenger's explanation: 'The Holy Spirit will come upon you, and the power of the Most High will overshadow you. So the holy one to be born will be called the Son of God' (Luke 1:26-35).

The story is one of the most beautiful, tender, touching accounts in all Scripture. We should read it – as Christians generally have read it – with a profound mixture of wonder, gratitude and great praise.

One of the important things Gabriel says in this annunciation of Jesus' birth is at the end. In fact, it is the very last words he utters. Mary has asked her question.

Gabriel has told her about the conception of Jesus by the Holy Spirit, adding a word about the impending birth of John the Baptist to Mary's cousin Elizabeth. Then he says, presumably in summary, 'For nothing is impossible with God' (v. 37).

Nothing! Nothing at all!

Those words are appropriate at the start of the Christmas story, and for us as we look back on it. In fact, they are appropriate for the entire gospel and for Christianity as a whole.

Four 'Impossibilities'

Mary needed to hear these words, which is why Gabriel spoke them, for she was being asked to believe things which, from a human perspective, were impossible.

The first was the Virgin Birth.

Unlike Elizabeth, who was old and barren but who nevertheless had a husband, Mary was unmarried and, as she testified to the angel, 'a virgin'. She was being asked to believe that she would conceive a child without intercourse. This apparent impossibility loomed so large in the thinking of some liberals in the last and at the beginning of this century that for them denial of the Virgin Birth became a test of theological respectability and even rationality. These men did not see how a miracle of this magnitude could be credited. Never mind that it had been confessed by the Church through many long centuries! Never mind that the miraculous birth is taught clearly not only in Luke but in Matthew also, and that it is alluded to in other places in Scripture! It was judged to be 'impossible'.

This was not the only 'impossibility' presented to Mary. Involved also was the far more overwhelming matter of the Incarnation. The Incarnation meant that God was to become man, which the angel indicated when he referred

88

to the one who was to be born as 'the holy one' and as 'the Son of God'. These terms could not have been used of any mere mortal.

What an 'impossibility' this was! It seemed as impossible to the Jews as to anybody, of course. But it seemed particularly impossible to the Greeks, to whom the gospel of the Incarnation later spread. In Greek philosophy the principle that most distinguished between God and man was that God was spirit while man was a combination of spirit and flesh (or matter). Spirit was good; flesh was evil. For Greek thinkers, this dichotomy explained how humans can aspire to noble thoughts and good actions while at the same time somehow always failing to achieve them.

This understanding also made acceptance of a doctrine such as the Incarnation impossible. For what would be involved if the Incarnation were true, according to Greek philosophy? God would have to link up with evil, wouldn't he? He would have to become bad. Since this is impossible if God is to remain God, so also is the Incarnation. According to the Greek way of thinking, salvation must be provided not by God becoming man but by man becoming God. Man has to escape the curse of bodily existence.

A third 'impossibility' may not have been in Mary's mind at this time – we do not know – but it is suggested by something she says in her great psalm of praise called *The Magnificat*, which follows just a bit further on in this chapter. Mary says, 'My spirit rejoices in God my Saviour' (v. 47). This is what the birth of Jesus was about, of course: salvation! But how is that possible? How can a holy God save sinners?

This was the problem fixed upon some years later by the enemies of Mary's child when they confronted the grown Jesus with the woman who had been taken in adultery. She was a sinner, they said. They had witnesses.

And Moses in the law had commanded that such a person should be stoned to death. What did Jesus say? Should they stone her, thus fulfilling the law of God? Or should they be merciful – Jesus had a reputation for being merciful – and let her go? These men were blind to the fact that in God's sight they too were sinners, no less than the woman was. But though they were blind to their own sin, they had nevertheless, with fiendish wisdom, hit upon a real problem. God is just. His law rightly demands punishment for sin. The woman *was* a sinner. She must be punished. Of course, Jesus wanted to be merciful! Don't we all? But the law must be upheld. How can one (even God) be merciful and uphold the law too?

As the gospel unfolds, we find that the answer is in the atonement: the righteous Son of God dies for sinners. But at the beginning this was not clear, and the problem was a big one. Shortly after this, when Mary's pregnancy became known and her fiance Joseph was preparing to break off the engagement, the angel appeared to him, explained the situation and announced that the child to be born was to be given the name Jesus, 'because he will save his people from their sins' (Matt. 1:21). But how? How could he do it? How could such a great impossibility become possible?

The final 'impossibility' is that salvation requires a change in people's hearts, and the hearts of men and women are hard. It is one thing for God to provide a way of salvation, however he might choose to do it. But why should Mary suppose that human beings would receive it? Mary knew the psalms. Psalm 14 declares,

'The LORD looks down from heaven
　　on the sons of men
to see if there are any who understand,
　　any who seek God.
All have turned aside,
　　they have together become corrupt;

90

there is no one who does good,
    not even one' (vv. 2, 3).

If the heart is as hard as the Bible declares it to be, how can we hope that anyone will respond to the Saviour and be saved?

God of the Impossible

But listen to the angel as he speaks these words to Mary. 'Nothing is impossible with God.' Nothing at all!

Or, for that matter, listen to what Jesus says later on in the gospel. A rich young ruler had come to Jesus asking what he needed to do to be saved, and Jesus had replied after some conversation that the man's riches were standing in his way. In his case, salvation required that he give up his riches, distribute them to the poor, and then follow Jesus. When the man turned away sorrowfully, Jesus reflected on the situation, saying, 'How hard it is for the rich to enter the kingdom of God! Indeed it is easier for a camel to go through the eye of a needle than for a rich man to enter the kingdom of God.'

For once the disciples were perceptive, recognizing that the problem they had just witnessed was not only for rich people but was a problem for all. So they asked in amazement, 'Who then can be saved?'

Jesus replied in words that echoed Gabriel's: 'What is impossible with men is possible with God' (Luke 18:18-27; cf. Matt. 19:26; Mark 10:27).

Why? Because God is not a man that he should be bound by our human limits or constraints. That is why in Christianity we stress that in the final analysis we are not dealing with psychology or sociology or mere good works or anything else that is simply human when we present the gospel, but with the reality of a world beyond, above and greater than our own. We are dealing with God. In other words, we do not live in a closed universe, where the cosmos is all there is, as Carl Sagan says, but in a universe in which the infinite God is the ultimate and determinate reality.

Do you remember the first motion picture based on the television series Star Trek? It was called Star Trek: The Motion Picture. In this movie an unknown, destructive power was coming toward earth, and the Enterprise was sent to intercept it. There was an encounter, and the invader eventually identified its mission as a quest 'for its creator'. That sounds religious, since everyone expected its creator to be God. But when the Enterprise crew uncovered what the invading power really was, they discovered that it was a lost American satellite that had somehow acquired additional powers of its own since its launching centuries earlier. When it came searching for 'its creator', it was searching for man, which meant that man was his own god. Inevitably so, if there is no reality beyond the universe!

In a world like this, man has no one to look to but himself, and nothing is miraculous. But Christianity does not agree with this. Christians do not believe in a closed universe. We believe that the universe has been created by God and that God stands behind and over it so that, from our perspective, intervention in this world by God is not only possible, it is to be expected.

A Virgin Birth? Why not? God is not bound by the laws of human intercourse and conception. God made the laws. He can operate within them or outside of them. With God all things are possible.

An Incarnation? Of course! God made man in his image originally. He can take man to himself through the birth of Jesus. And he need not contaminate himself with evil or sin in doing so, as the Greeks thought, since flesh is not evil in itself. God made our flesh. It has become sinful only through our rebellion against God.

The salvation of the race? The atonement is God's answer to this seemingly insurmountable problem.

And man's hard heart? God can change the heart. He can change hearts as easily as he can change the winds. In fact, he is able to make the heart over again, which is what Jesus told Nicodemus when he said, 'You must be born again' (John 3:7). Jesus said, 'The wind blows wherever it pleases. You hear its sound, but you cannot tell where it comes from or where it is going. So it is with everyone born of the Spirit' (v. 8).

All Things Possible
It would be a wrong application of this text to say that you and I are to have miracles in our lives comparable to the Virgin Birth or the Incarnation. By definition, those are one-of-a-kind events. Jesus came into this world by human birth once. He will not return that way again.

But we need to apply the text, nevertheless – if only because these words (or their equivalents) are used in a more general way elsewhere in Scripture. With God it was possible even for the rich young man to have believed. That is an area for application. Or, as Jesus said when he was confronted with a boy who was possessed by an evil spirit and was asked to heal him, 'Everything is possible for him who believes' (Mark 9:23). That is, it is possible for the one who believes God's promises.

In what areas today can we apply the words of the angel to Mary? What can we believe is possible for us, even though it seems impossible by human standards?

Let me suggest two answers.

(1) *Anything God promises in his Word is possible, regardless of how impossible it may seem to you now.* More than that, it is certain, for God does not cheat on his promises. He does not break his word. As Matthew Henry says, 'No

word of God must be incredible to us, as long as no work of God is impossible to him.'[1]

I feel sorry for people who do not know the Bible, because their ignorance deprives them of the comfort it provides. Much of this is expressed in the Bible's promises:

> For God so loved the world that he gave his one and only Son, that whoever believes in him shall not perish but have eternal life (John 3:16).

> I am the gate; whoever enters through me will be saved (John 10:9).

> Come to me, all you who are weary and burdened, and I will give you rest. Take my yoke upon you and learn from me, for I am gentle and humble in heart, and you will find rest for your souls. For my yoke is easy and my burden is light (Matt. 11:28-30).

> Do not be anxious about anything, but in everything, by prayer and petition, with thanksgiving, present your requests to God. And the peace of God, which transcends all understanding, will guard your hearts and your minds in Christ Jesus (Phil. 4:6, 7).

> My God will meet all your needs according to his glorious riches in Christ Jesus (Phil. 4:19).

I like something the great English Bishop J. C. Ryle said about our text and God's promises. He wrote,

> There is no sin too black and bad to be pardoned. The blood of Christ cleanseth from all sin. There is no heart too hard and wicked to be changed. The heart of

---

[1] Matthew Henry, *Commentary on the Whole Bible*, Vol. 5, *Matthew to John* (New York, London and Edinburgh: Fleming H. Revell, n.d.), p. 565. Original edition 1721.

stone can be made a heart of flesh. There is no work too hard for a believer to do. We may do all things through Christ strengthening us. There is no trial too hard to be borne. The grace of God is sufficient for us. There is no promise too great to be fulfilled. Christ's words never pass away, and what he has promised he is able to perform. There is no difficulty too great for a believer to overcome. When God is for us, who shall be against us? The mountain shall become a plain. [2]

(2) *God's plan for your life is possible, even though it seems at times that what God is asking you to do is not.* Our problem here is that we usually confuse our plans with God's plan for us, and when we have trouble achieving our own goals we begin to doubt God's ability. We must learn that God's ways are not our ways, that his ways are best, and learn to trust him. The Bible says,

> Trust in the LORD with all your heart
> and lean not on your own understanding;
> in all your ways acknowledge him,
> and he will make your paths straight (Prov. 3:5, 6)

I recognize that God may have placed you in a very difficult situation.

You may be married to a beast of a husband or to a profligate wife. You know that the Bible says that you are not to seek to separate from your spouse, but you do not know how you can obey it. You are tempted to think that the requirements of God are impossible. They are not impossible. God will give you strength to do what he says is right.

You may have lost a husband or a wife, one you loved very much. Now you are alone. It is Christmas, and the

---

[2] John Charles Ryle, *Expository Thoughts on the Gospels: St. Luke*, vol. 1 (Cambridge: James Clarke & Co., 1976), pp. 28, 29.

memories of past holidays rise up to make you sad. You wonder how you can continue alone. Suppose you have to go on for another ten or twenty years? If God has put you in that situation, it is because he has something still left for you to do. He will help you do it. It may seem impossible, but with God all things are possible. God is not finished with you yet.

You may be facing a difficult situation at work. Your boss may be abusive, or a fellow-worker may be out to get you. You do not know how you can remain in the job, let alone continue to behave like a Christian under such hard circumstances. It is not impossible. Christians have suffered under worse circumstances and have continued to bear a sound testimony. God will help you.

Perhaps your work is boring. You have been stuffing the same dull products into the same dull boxes day after day for years. Or you have been typing the same monotonous invoices or letters. At one point you hoped you would be promoted to something better, but someone else always got the better job and now you are resigned to staying in exactly the same spot until retirement. You wonder how you can keep going on. God will enable you. What is more, he will make your work-place a fruitful spot to be, if you will let him. He will make you attractive so that, even though the work is repetitive and uninteresting, you will be interesting and others will be attracted to you. You will find pleasure in what God is doing through you to help others.

Perhaps you are facing an overwhelming challenge at work. The task seems impossible, and you know that there are people who are waiting for you to fail so they can get rid of you and perhaps take your place. If God has given you your task, your task is not impossible. God will work through you. He will accomplish his plan for your life.

Suppose you fail? Then, that is what he has ordained for you, and you will find even in the failure that God is still good.

In the final analysis, how can any of us fail, since the goal of our lives is to be made into the image of Jesus Christ and God has promised to do that with us. That is why the Apostle Paul wrote, 'We know that in all things God works for the good of those who love him' (Rom. 8:28). It is why he could say, 'I have learned the secret of being content in any and every situation, whether well fed or hungry, whether living in plenty or in want. I can do everything through him who gives me strength' (Phil. 4:12, 13).

The Servant of the Lord

But you need to accept what God is doing with you, and I mean accept it willingly, not fighting against it. Think back to Gabriel's annunciation of the birth of Jesus to Mary. I said earlier that the words 'nothing is impossible with God' were the last words Gabriel spoke, and that is true! But they are not the last words of the story. Immediately after Gabriel said those words, Mary responded, 'I am the Lord's servant. May it be to me as you have said' (v. 38).

Isn't that wonderful? Those words were not easy to say. Submission to God exposed Mary to a blemished reputation, loss of her engagement to Joseph, danger and possibly even death. Adulterers could be stoned. But Mary said, 'I am the Lord's servant. May it be to me as you have said.'

That is the secret of a happy and fruitful life. If we go our own way, we shall be like lost sheep, far from home, frustrated and helpless. But if we respond like Mary, we shall be blessed by God. And who knows what God will yet do with us?

When Mary submitted herself to God, God sent the Saviour.

PART THREE

THE BIRTH

8

GOD'S TIME FULLY COME

(Galatians 4:4-5)

But when the time had fully come, God sent his Son, born of a woman, born under law, to redeem those under law, that we might receive the full rights of sons.

Quite a few years ago, when I was a student studying for the ministry at Princeton Theological Seminary, I worked on Sundays in a church that was in a nearby community. I remember that as Christmas got close that year, on one occasion the senior pastor and I were talking about Christmas and he complained to me, 'I don't know what in the world I'm going to preach on for Christmas this year.'

I was a bit brash at the time, as young men are. So I replied rather quickly, 'Why don't you preach on Galatians 4:4, 5, on God sending Christ in the fullness of time.'

He said, 'That's the first thing every young preacher preaches on when he gets into a church.' And that was the end of that conversation.

Well, the years went by. I completed my own study. I came to Tenth Presbyterian Church in Philadelphia and began preaching on different Christmas themes – for quite a number of years, it seems to me. And one year, as I was looking at verses on which I might speak at Christmas, I came across this text and remembered that conversation years ago. It occurred to me that in all those years I had never once turned to this obvious Christmas text: 'But when the time had fully come, God sent his Son, born of a woman, born under law, to redeem those under law, that we might receive the full rights of sons.'

In His Time
This is an interesting text and a very good one, especially as we think about the movement of God in history and what it means for us. It is a helpful corrective for the way we often think. Isn't it true that we tend to think of the great acts of God in history as being rather sudden.

Let me explain. If you are walking in the fields on a summer evening and a storm is brewing and all of a sudden, with no warning, there is a brilliant flash of lightning and a great clap of thunder, you say, 'Oh, look at the power of God.' It is the suddenness that makes us think of God. Or again, if you have a relative who is sick, has been taken to the hospital and seems to be declining, and then rather suddenly, there is a turnabout in his or her condition, you say, 'God intervened and healed this person.' Again, we have identified suddenness as the mark of God's handiwork.

Now, actually, the opposite is probably more often true. I do not mean to say that God cannot intervene suddenly, for, of course, he does. But as we look at all we know of God from Scripture and see of him in nature, we see the slow workings of God, his patience and the ordered timeliness of events most characterising his actions. Nature alone teaches that. We respond when lightning flashes. But God operates most characteristically by the slow building up of the mountains, the stretched-out development of trees and the regular unfolding of the seasons. Most of what God does in nature takes many, many years if not millennia.

We find the same thing in the Bible. When we turn to the Scriptures for the record of God's revelation of himself to men and women, we find that God did not reveal himself entirely and at once, in a flash. He revealed himself over many hundreds and even thousands of years, gradually building from basic, foundational revelations to those that were more complete and complex. The first rudimentary promise of the coming of Jesus Christ is in Genesis 3:15. It is a promise of one who will crush the head of Satan though his heel will be wounded in the process. To Abraham God revealed a little more, showing that the nations of the world should be blessed through him. David, Isaiah, Daniel, Micah, Malachi – all in turn received their additional piece of revelation until, in the end, Jesus Christ the eternal Son of God actually stood upon earth and eventually died and rose again for our salvation.

All of this happened in 'the fullness of time'. So the first thing we learn from that phrase, it seems to me, is to be patient and wait upon God, knowing that he never acts too soon, never comes too late; but rather, always does all things perfectly in his own perfect time.

There is a hymn that expresses this beautifully. It comes from the hymn-book of the great Keswick Convention of England.

Not so in haste, my heart;
Have faith in God and wait.
Although he linger long,
He never comes too late.

He never comes too late.
He knoweth what is best.
Vex not thyself in vain.
Until he cometh, rest.

Until he cometh, rest,
Nor grudge the hours that roll.
The feet that wait for God
Are soonest at the goal.

Are soonest at the goal
That is not gained by speed.
Then hold thee still, my heart,
For I shall wait his lead.

I want to look at the phrase 'God's time fully come' in three ways. First, I want to look at it as describing the world's time, that is, the progression of history. Secondly, I want to look at it as referring to God's time, that is, to the unfolding of the great drama of redemption. Thirdly, I want to look at it as relating to our time, which concerns our trusting God. In each case, we are going to see that it is in the fullness of time, that is, at exactly the right moment, that God operates.

The World's Time: History

First, it was in the fullness of historical time that the Lord Jesus Christ came to earth. I mean by this that God prepared history for the coming of Jesus Christ. Here are some of the ways he did it.

(1) *A Roman peace*. At the time of Christ's birth the civilised world of the day was united politically as it had not been for many centuries before. Caesar Augustus, who is mentioned in Luke's account of the Christmas story (Luke 2:1), is credited by historians as having established what came to be known as 'the pax Romana', the Roman peace. Until the triumph of Augustus, climaxing the Roman civil wars that unfolded upon the murder of Julius Caesar, the Mediterranean world was racked with disorder. There were pirates on the seas, warring factions

on the land, robbers on all the major roads, and even civil war within the Roman Empire itself. In addition, there was the continuing threat of destruction from the barbarians who were pressing in upon the empire from every side.

Augustus brought peace. So there was brought about, shortly before the time of the Lord Jesus Christ, a tranquillity in the world which was an obvious preparation for the coming of Jesus and the expanding proclamation of the gospel.

(2) *A system of roads.* The world was also linked together as it had not been previously. One obvious form of this was the Roman road or highway system. We have an expression which says, 'All roads lead to Rome,' and that was literally true in Augustus' day. Wherever the armies went, roads were built. The armies were great road builders, and they had a very peculiar way of making roads. For instance, if they came to a raised area they usually did not worry about going around it. They cut through. They never deviated from the straight and most direct line if they could help it. So when you see the remains of these great roads – as you can in Europe today, particularly in England – you find that they just set out straight across the country.

This magnificent system of roads literally linked all areas of the Roman Empire. So when the Apostle Paul and the other early missionaries began to take the gospel to that world, they found that the Roman roads were a great means of communication. As a matter of fact, it is possible to trace Paul's travels through Asia Minor by his apparently deliberate attempt to follow this road system.

(3) *A common language.* There was another way in which history had prepared for the coming of Jesus Christ, and this was the language that united the empire. The Romans, who spoke Latin, were in control, but the

language that united the empire was not Latin. It was Greek. Preparation for this marvellous unity began with the conquests of Alexander the Great. He had come from Macedonia, where his father Philip had been a powerful king before him, and he had pressed his conquest towards the east, first conquering the rest of Greece, then crossing the Hellespont into what we call Turkey, pressing on into Palestine and finally moving even further east until he came to the very borders of India. All that great area was settled by the descendants of Alexander the Great. So the Greek language that went with him soon became the political and business language of the ancient civilisations he conquered.

The Greeks did not press west in the same way as they had gone east. But the Greek language nevertheless conquered the west by commerce. The Greek ships sailed west, touching ports along the entire coasts of Italy and Sicily so that today, if you visit those areas of the world, you find extensive Greek remains. In fact, the largest number of Greek temples, the centres of the Greek cities, are to be found, not on the mainland of Greece or on the Greek islands, but in Italy. The greatest single collection of Greek temples anywhere in the world is south of Naples along the Italian coast.

Wherever Greek traders went, their language went also. So although Rome had conquered the world politically, the Greeks conquered the world in terms of Greek language, ideas and culture. Thus, when Paul went from place to place in the Empire, he did not have to learn all the hundreds of different dialects that were current. All he had to know was Greek.

(4) *A spiritual vacuum*. There was a fourth way the world was prepared for the coming of Jesus Christ, not in expectation but in desperation. The religions of

the ancient world had run their course. These religions focused on the gods and goddesses of the Greek and Roman pantheons. But they had proved meaningless by the time Christ was born. It was a situation similar to what we have in our day – people turning from the gods of their fathers to any god that comes along. There was a resurgence of the religions of the east and a general opening towards what they would have regarded as new truth or truth from any quarter. This too was God's preparation in history for the preaching of the Christian gospel.

So the first thing we are taught by Galatians 4:4, 5 is that it was in the fullness of the world's time that God sent his Son to be the Saviour.

God's Time: Redemption
There is a second way in which we need to look at the fullness of time, however, and it is this: not as the fullness of the world's time, that is, as history, but as the fullness of God's time. We can hardly miss this when we look at the context of these verses, because Galatians is not talking about what had happened in Rome, Greece or even Israel prior to the coming of Jesus Christ, but rather of what God was doing in the unfolding drama of redemption. Paul is talking about the contrast between Old Testament times and the time introduced by Christ's coming. He is saying, 'Your situation now is better than it was before, because God, in the fullness of time, has brought the plan of salvation to its culmination.'

(1) *Shadow and substance.* One way in which the old was superseded was that the substance replaced the shadow. I do not mean to say that in Old Testament times, nobody ever understood that Christ was coming or had a clear perception of who he would be and what he was to do.

Abraham had considerable understanding, and so did David and the prophets and undoubtedly others.

But, generally speaking, the coming of Jesus Christ and the significance of his ministry were hidden in the shadows of the Old Testament system. The people obediently made sacrifices, but the reality was somewhat hidden in this shadow. All the sacrifices pointed forwards to the reality which was Jesus Christ. He was the true and only sufficient sacrifice. The people had the temple worship, but the temple worship was symbolic at every point, teaching how men and women would ultimately approach God through the Lord Jesus Christ. Jesus was symbolised by the brazen altar in the courtyard of the temple, the great laver in the courtyard, the showbread within the Holy Place, the seven-branched candlestick. Above all, he was symbolised by the Mercy Seat of the Ark of the Covenant which pointed to his coming atonement for sin.

All these things were only shadows in the Old Testament period. But now, in the fullness of God's time, they have been revealed and brought to glorious fulfilment by the coming of Christ.

(2) *Laws and liberty*. Moreover – and this is the theme of Galatians – those who believe in Christ have entered into the full liberty of the children of God so that they are no longer under the Old Testament laws, rules and regulations.

I need to be careful at this point, because whenever one speaks about Christians being free from the law there are always some who suppose this means that a Christian can do as he pleases. That is, if there is no law, we can sin as we will. This is the heresy of Antinomianism, and it is not what Paul is teaching. Paul does indeed teach that we are not under law, but we are not under law only because we have passed on to a greater maturity and a higher responsibility.

Paul illustrates his teaching by speaking of a minor child, who is placed under tutors who dictate what the child shall do and not do until he comes of age. However when he comes of age and is a man in his own right, he is no longer under tutors but rather is free to exercise his own personal responsibility and thus honour his father by what he does. Paul says that this is what has happened to us since the coming of Jesus Christ. Formerly we were under the Old Testament laws and regulations. But now we are free to serve God as responsible men and women.

So as we talk about the fullness of time, we also rejoice at the fullness of God's redemption. True, the world was prepared for Christ's coming. There was a fullness of time there. But there was an even greater fullness of time in the history of God's eternal plan.

Our Time: Trusting God
My third point is that there is a fullness of time in which Christ comes to each of us. This gives us confidence in evangelism. If converting men and women depended upon the preacher or the one who is witnessing, who could bear such a burden? We would be anxious, worried, distressed, distraught, thinking that perhaps if we do not speak exactly the right word or do so at exactly the right time, the person to whom we are speaking will be lost. But it is not that way. God comes in the fullness of time to each heart.

Paul referred to this, using the illustration of planting, growth and harvest. He said in reference to himself and Apollos, 'I planted the seed, Apollos watered it, but God made it grow. So neither he who plants nor he who waters is anything, but only God, who makes things grow' (1 Cor. 3:6, 7). This is the way it is in evangelism. God begins to work in a heart. He does so through sowing the seed of his Word. At the beginning it may be such a small seed that you hardly know the plant is there. But the Word of God is present and growing. Then somebody else comes along and waters it a little, and there is some more growth. From beginning to end the work is God's who causes each of his ministers to contribute what is needed in the proper fullness of time.

I wonder if that is the way it is with you. There may be somebody who has sown the seed of the gospel in your heart. One person has explained the gospel to you. Another has witnessed to the reality of Christ's power from his or her own experience with God. A third has answered your questions. A minister has taught you from the Bible through faithful exposition. But you have not yet come to the point at which you have made a personal, believing response to Jesus Christ.

I wonder if that time might be now.

What better time than now! I cannot say, in your particular case, that this is the time. But I can warn you against delaying beyond the time God has established. Perhaps God is saying, 'Jesus, who came two thousand years ago and was born in a manger, also died on the cross. And the man who died on the cross died for you. He died in your place, for your sin. After that he rose again and now lives for ever and works to draw people just like you to faith in himself as the Saviour. I want you to abandon your sinful way of life and follow him.'

If God is saying those things to you and is calling you to follow Jesus, whom you have heard about and know a great deal about already, then this is the time, the fullness of time, for you to make a commitment.

Say, 'Lord Jesus Christ, I acknowledge my need of you as my Saviour, and I commit myself to you. I promise to follow you from this time onward and for

ever.' I hope you will do that if you have never done it
before.

He Is Coming Again

Let me add one final point. I can hardly leave it out. In the
fullness of time Jesus Christ will come again. It was when
'the time was fully come' that the Lord Jesus Christ came
the first time. And in just the same way, it will be in 'the
fullness of time' that he will come back.

I do not know when that will be. I do not see things
as God sees them. I do not know when all the harvest of
God's people will be gathered in. But I know that Peter
wrote about it in his second letter, saying,

> In the last days scoffers will come, scoffing and
> following their own evil desires. They will say, 'Where
> is this "coming" he promised? Ever since our fathers
> died, everything goes on as it has since the beginning
> of creation ... Do not forget this one thing, dear friends.
> With the Lord a day is like a thousand years, and a
> thousand years are like a day. The Lord is not slow in
> keeping his promise, as some understand slowness. He
> is patient with you, not wanting anyone to perish, but
> everyone to come to repentance' (2 Pet. 3:3, 4, 8, 9).

Jesus will return when the fullness of the harvest has been
brought in.

The point is: Will you be ready for him when he returns?
I do not know when that will be. It may be far off. It may
be soon. It could be right now. Are you ready?

The Lord Jesus Christ came the first time to die. The
second time he will come as a King to rule and as a Judge
to reward everyone according to what he or she has done
– whether it be good or bad. Can you stand before him on
the basis of what you have done? Can you say, 'Lord Jesus
Christ, look at my good works. See how good they are.

Take me into heaven. I am as good as you are'? Or must you be exposed in your sin and be eternally ashamed before him at his coming? The only way to stand is in the righteousness of Christ, which God offers you if you will turn from your sin and believe on Jesus.

God is never rushed. Jesus will not come too soon. He will not come too late. And the proof of that is that he did not come either too soon or too late the first time. I trust that he will come to you now and that you, for your part, might come to him.

9

THE BIRTH OF THE SAVIOUR
(Luke 2:1-20)

In those days Caesar Augustus issued a decree that a census should be taken of the entire Roman world. (This was the first census that took place while Quirinius was governor of Syria.) And everyone went to his own town to register.

So Joseph also went up from the town of Nazareth in Galilee to Judea, to Bethlehem the town of David, because he belonged to the house and line of David. He went there to register with Mary, who was pledged to be married to him and was expecting a child. While they were there, the time came for the baby to be born, and she gave birth to her firstborn, a son. She wrapped him in cloths and placed him in a manger, because there was no room for them in the inn.

And there were shepherds living out in the fields nearby, keeping watch over their flocks at night. An angel of the Lord appeared to them, and the glory of the Lord shone around them, and they were terrified. But the angel said to them, 'Do not be afraid. I bring you good news of great joy that will be for all the people. Today in the town of David a Saviour has been born to you; he is Christ the Lord. This will be a sign to you: You will find a baby wrapped in cloths and lying in a manger.'

Suddenly a great company of the heavenly host appeared with the angel, praising God and saying,

'Glory to God in the highest,
    and on earth peace to men on whom his favour
        rests.'

When the angels had left them and gone into heaven, the shepherds said to one another, 'Let's go to Bethlehem and see this thing that has happened, which the Lord has told us about.'

So they hurried off and found Mary and Joseph, and the baby, who was lying in the manger. When they had seen him, they spread the word concerning what had been told them about this child, and all who heard it were amazed at what the shepherds said to them. But Mary treasured up all these things and pondered them in her heart. The shepherds returned, glorifying and praising God for all the things they had heard and seen, which were just as they had been told.

Birthdays are usually happy times – when people remember them. For that reason we generally try to memorise the birthdays of close friends. We always remember the birthdays of children, because the children remind us. When we get older, we are supposed to be too sophisticated to remind people that our birthdays are coming, but we are still pleased when they recollect. Very old people are especially glad when their birthdays are remembered. I know many who count the cards that come to them, and it pleases them to say how many of their friends recalled their special day.

Of all the birthdays that are recollected, however, there is no birthday that has ever been remembered more faithfully or by more people over a longer period of time than the birthday of Jesus Christ. And it is not merely Christian people who remember it. We would expect that of those who, by the grace of God, are following Jesus as their Saviour and Lord and are trying to serve him. The remarkable thing is that the birthday of Jesus Christ is also remembered by non-Christian people. They even seem to have a sentimental attachment to the story.

The Christmas specials on television contain much material that is easily forgettable. There is much we probably should not even see. But sometimes, even in the worst of these programmes, there will be a little segment where people get serious and someone will at least talk about the birth of Jesus or even recite a portion of the Christmas chapters.

What is there about this story, what is there about the birth of Christ that so fixes itself upon the minds of our contemporaries and will no doubt continue to enthral the minds of those who come after us?

There are a number of answers, of course. Some would say, 'It's the sentimentality of the story.' Others would say, 'It's a religious story, one of the best, and people are always kind of religious.' Those may be partial answers, but I think there is more to it than that. I think the story comes across to us in a powerful way because of the extraordinary incongruities or paradoxes in the story. There are things you would not expect to find and yet do find, and it is these that make the story particularly memorable.

Incongruities and Paradoxes

It is easy to think of some of them. The Christmas story is about purity and godliness in an unwed mother. Under any other circumstances, this would be the kind of thing people might joke about or refer to by snide remarks. Yet there is not a breath of that in the story. Instead, there is an aura of holiness over it, as Mary, who is with child by

115

the Holy Spirit, says, 'How will this be?' (Luke 1:34), and God explains it to her.

Or again, the Christmas story is about joy in what could have been a tragedy. In Judaism at this time, to commit fornication and to have the evidence of it in the early arrival of a child was a bad thing. In fact, it was a crime punishable in some instances by stoning. This is what Joseph was afraid of when he determined not to make Mary's condition public but 'to divorce her quietly' (Matt. 1:19). Yet God himself overshadowed the story so that even Mary, who is faced with the problem, rejoices in the Lord and goes off to see Elizabeth, and they have that moving exchange between them, in which Elizabeth blesses Mary, and Mary breaks forth into the magnificent hymn we know as *The Magnificat*.

Of all these paradoxes of the story, however, the one that is most apparent and comes across in the clearest way to everyone is that the King of kings, the very Lord of glory, came in humble circumstances and is presented to us in his first moments upon earth in a manger. His mother and Joseph have come to Bethlehem, where he was to be born. Crowds fill the city. There is no place for them to stay. So they find the only available shelter in a stable, and it is there, where the animals are housed, in the most humble of all circumstances, that the King of glory is born. There is something about that circumstance that touches the heart and speaks eloquently of the humility of God who would come down to our level and associate with us in this way. The paradox did not escape the biblical writers, of course, and it was perfectly evident to Luke, who actually highlights it as he tells the story.

A Downward Progression

I wonder if you have ever noticed that, as Luke begins to tell the story, he establishes a certain downward progression from the supposedly important people of the world to those who, in the eyes of the world, were not important characters at all.

Look at verse 1: 'In those days Caesar Augustus...' Now there is the place to begin if you want to tell a good story. It's like saying 'In the days of George Washington' or anybody else that you think is important. An important name is certain to demand attention, and that is what Luke is doing here. By beginning with Caesar Augustus, he begins his account with the most important person of that age.

Augustus had brought the *pax Romana* or Roman peace. As a result of Julius Caesar's fateful decision to cross the Rubicon river and thus defy the decree of the Roman senate, the great general was eventually assassinated and civil war engulfed the Roman Empire. The wars were between Mark Anthony, on the one hand, and Brutus and Cacius, on the other. In the end Anthony was the victor, but then there were wars between Anthony and Augustus. For twenty years the Roman Empire was torn by civil war. But when the great Augustus finally gained the throne, he ruled so well and extended his power in such a thorough way that a time of welcome and much-applauded peace ensued. Augustus put down insurrections, sealed the empire's borders against the barbarians and cleared the Mediterranean Sea of pirates.

That was Caesar Augustus. So when Luke begins his story by saying, 'In those days Caesar Augustus...,' he begins at the top, and everybody who reads his story would know that this is precisely what he is doing.

The next person mentioned is 'Quirinius, the governor of Syria' (v. 2). Quirinius was also a very important person. To be a governor of a Roman province was an important job. Furthermore, the governor of Syria was close at hand since Syria was just to the north of Judea and would therefore be well known to the people of the south. Yet Quirinius was still only a governor. He was not the emperor. So we can see that Luke was deliberately stepping down a bit when he mentions him.

Then we come to verse 4, which says, 'So Joseph....' Here is the third character in the story. He is a male Jew, which was important. He was also a descendant of the great King David, which was very important; he was in the royal line. Yet Joseph was a poor man, and, of course, he was a member of a race whose people had been overcome by Rome. Joseph was insignificant in the eyes of the Romans, and probably to his fellow Jews as well.

Luke comes to Mary in verse 5: 'He went there to register with Mary, who was pledged to be married to him and was expecting a child.' Mary was a woman, therefore, in the way of thinking of the time, even less significant than Joseph. Women were always thought to be insignificant. Besides, she was as poor as he was, and she was expecting a child.

Finally, after Luke has gone through this meaningful list of names, from Caesar Augustus to Quirinius to Joseph to Mary, at the very end of the story he comes to the child, Mary's firstborn son, whom she wrapped in strips of cloth and placed in a manger. How insignificant can one be – a child of a poor family, born in a distant, occupied area of the Roman Empire? Yet the irony of the story – the paradox at this point – is that this baby, Mary's infant, the insignificant, poor child of that poor couple, was none other than the Lord of glory, even the Son of God himself. Luke was very aware of that irony, and he is calling attention to it by writing along these lines.

No Room In The Inn
There is a second related paradox in the story, and it is the fact that when Mary and Joseph came to Bethlehem

there was no place for them. There was no room in the inn. When Luke says that, we have to understand that there was no room for them anywhere, because if there had been any other place for them, they would have gone there. Inns were rough and not very reputable places. So when they could not even get into the inn and ended up in a stable, this is the equivalent of saying that there was no place for them at all. No place at all! Even though the child Mary was carrying was the Son of God.

That is worth thinking about.

For one thing, it shows that there was no room for this couple and their newborn child in the homes of the mighty. Luke has just mentioned Caesar Augustus, but there was no room for Christ in Caesar's palace. Caesar did not know of the birth, but even if he had, he certainly would never have taken this poor couple in. There was no room for this family with Quirinius, whom Luke has also mentioned. Quirinius would not have bothered. There just was no room among the mighty.

There was no room among the philosophers either. If this family had been in Greece and had appeared in the agora (place of assembly) before the wise men of Greece and had made their need known there, none of the philosophers would have received them.

Perhaps the Jews would have done better, we think, if they had only known. But they did not do better. Were there no good families in Bethlehem that could have taken them in? After all, Joseph was a descendant of King David. He was related to some if not most of these people. Wouldn't some of these good families have taken them in? No. It is usually the case that good families take care of good families. They do not take care of those who do not come from good families. The rich care for the rich. They do not care for the poor, which was the case with Joseph.

We are inclined to think that those sad days have passed. Today is quite different, we say. Certainly if Jesus were around now, people would make room for him. But, no, as a matter of fact, he would receive the same reception today as he received then. It is because the hearts of men and women are the same today as they have been in the past. It is true that Jesus was an infant then, and the rejection of the family in that day was somewhat different from the way he is rejected today. Then it was a case of gross insensitivity to an expecting mother's need. But it is not much different today, unless, of course, it is worse, because we now know who Jesus Christ is and what he stands for. Jesus is the Son of God who exposes and condemns sin and claims to be the only way of salvation. People do not want that message today any more than they wanted the infant Jesus then.

People get sentimental at Christmas and are inclined to say, 'We would receive Christ.' But they do not receive him unless God first does a work of regeneration in their hearts and thus leads them to do it.

Do You Have Room?

So here is an application: Do *you* have room for Jesus Christ? We have a hymn that says,

Come to my heart, Lord Jesus.
There is room in my heart for thee.

But is there room in your heart for Jesus? Or is he, and are his claims, crowded out by other matters?

They can be crowded out by your own conception of yourself. You say, 'I am what I am and do what I want to do. I want to do things my way. If Jesus has some other idea in mind, he will just have to give it up, because I am going to do my own thing.'

Jesus and his claims can also be crowded out by your pre-occupation with things. Americans are especially guilty of this, and at no time are we more guilty than at Christmas. We concentrate on the many things we want. That is where our hearts and minds are really focused, and Jesus gets pushed aside.

Is there room in your heart for Jesus? If Jesus is God's great gift to humanity, as we say, then you could never have anything greater in your life than Jesus. All true blessing begins with receiving him. Yet foolishly we try to keep him out.

Angels and Shepherds
A third striking paradox of the Christmas story is the announcement of the birth of Jesus to the shepherds. Why shepherds? I do not have an answer to that except that they were insignificant people, people who were looked down upon, and the gospel is for all such people. Shepherds were so poorly regarded that according to Jewish law, they were not even allowed to give testimony in a court of law because it was assumed they would lie. There was nothing romantic or glorious about shepherds. Yet it was to shepherds that the announcement of the birth of Jesus was made.

And by whom? By angels, by the heralds of heaven. We might think that if the angels came to earth to speak to anybody, it should have been to Caesar or Quirinius or the Jewish authorities. But that is not what they did. God gave this glorious announcement to despised men who were out in the fields with their sheep. And, you know, the experience they had was not even shared by the parents of the child. True, an angel had appeared to Joseph to tell him how to name the child and to Mary with the announcement of his birth. But I do not read in the story that Mary and Joseph heard the angels sing.

If God made the news of this gospel known to the shepherds, those who were at the absolute bottom of the social order of the day, then God is making that announcement known to everybody. He is making it known to you, whoever you may be or whatever you may have done. From the highest to the lowest, the glory of the gospel is revealed to all who are lost in sin, so that by the grace of God we might be lifted out of sin and be made like Jesus Christ.

The Proper Response
I notice something else at the end of the story. I call it instructions on how to celebrate the birth of Christ rightly, matters in which the outcast shepherds and Mary lead the way. There are four items: the witness of the shepherds, the response of those who heard their message, Mary's reaction to these things, and a final description of what the shepherds did.

(1) *Proclamation.* Verse 17 says, 'When they had seen him, they spread the word concerning what had been told them about this child.' This means that the shepherds became witnesses to what they had seen, and I conclude from this that the best way to celebrate Christmas is to make this marvellous story known. Why did the shepherds do that? They had not been told to do it. They had not been commissioned to be witnesses. Who were they to go around telling what had been told them about this child?

You know the answer. They did not need a special command or commission. The world was there, and the world desperately needed to hear that message. Since they had the message they did the natural thing. They told everyone they met what had happened.

(2) *Amazement.* Verse 18 says, 'All who heard it were amazed at what the shepherds said to them.' Isn't it true that even today there is something eternally amazing and truly wonderful about Christmas? It is why Christmas is

often oriented towards children; children wonder at what they see. As we get older we sometimes cease to wonder, but we are the losers for it. We should respond to Christmas by recapturing the wonder of these events.

(3) *Pondering*. Verse 19 says, 'Mary treasured up all these things and pondered them in her heart.' This is beyond mere amazement. A person can be amazed at something, but if that amazement lacks content, the amazement alone does not carry us very far. Mary was amazed, no doubt. But she went further than this by remembering what had happened and by trying to figure it out or understand it.

If you imitate Mary in this, it will involve some hard work. I notice that in this case it involved memory, because Mary 'treasured' up all these things. That is, she remembered them. It involved the affections, because she treasured them up 'in her heart'. Finally, it involved her intellect, because she 'pondered' them. That is, she tried to figure them out. There are many things in Christianity that are hard to understand: the Trinity, providence, the incarnation, many other doctrines. I suppose we will never understand any of these things fully, but that does not mean that we are not to try to understand them. Our minds should be stretched by these things, especially by the birth of Jesus Christ, and we should think about them deeply.

(4) *Praise*. Verse 20 says, 'The shepherds returned, glorifying and praising God for all the things they had heard and seen, which were just as they had been told.' This means that the shepherds did not only speak to men, giving a testimony; they also spoke to God, praising and glorifying him. They were saying, 'What a great God you are to come to us in such a way!'

I think that is what we should do also.

But I suggest that if you are having trouble with these things, the place to begin is not so much with speaking to others, but with the second, third and fourth points: amazement, pondering, and praising and glorifying God. Because when you have done that, and God and his gospel have a proper hold on your heart, then you will find it easy to talk to others and so spread the great good news about the incarnation.

This is a tremendous story. It is filled with wonderful incongruities. But it comes down to this: that God has entered human life at the lowest possible level so that everybody, whether low or high, openly sinful or self-righteous, may be included. Jesus is for you, whoever you are. Won't you receive him into your heart as your Saviour?

10

AN ASTONISHING REVELATION[1]

(Luke 2:11)

Today in the town of David a Saviour has been born to
you; he is Christ the Lord.

It is not usual or even wise to start a Christmas message
with a detail of Greek grammar, but I am going to do
that in this chapter because the heart of the angel's message
to the shepherds about the birth of Jesus depends upon
it. The shepherds were afraid when they saw the angel,
probably even more so when the greater host of angels
appeared. But the angel told them, 'Do not be afraid.
I bring you good news of great joy that will be for all the
people. Today in the town of David a Saviour has been
born to you; he is Christ the Lord' (Luke 2:10, 11).

The point of grammar I want to make is in the last three
words. 'Christ' and 'Lord' are both in the nominative case,
which means they are equated. The reason this is important
and so wonderful is that we might have expected 'Lord,'
the second of the two words, to be in the genitive case.

If that were the situation, the sentence would read,
'Today in the town of David a Saviour has been born to

---

[1] Parts of this chapter have been borrowed from James Montgomery Boice,
'Jesus Christ Our Lord' (Romans 1:4) in *Romans*, vol. 1 (Grand Rapids: Baker
Book House, 1992).

you; he is the Lord's Christ [Messiah].' I have said that this statement might have been expected because it is true – Jesus is God's Messiah – and also because that is exactly what the people of that day, including the shepherds, were expecting. They were expecting God to send the Messiah. But when the angel announced his birth, by a subtle change from the genitive to the nominative case, the angel proclaimed the newborn child not only to be 'the Lord's Anointed' but 'The Anointed One who *is* the Lord'. In other words, it was a statement not only of his function but of his nature. It meant that the baby was divine.

Jesus is Jehovah

I emphasise this because the words 'Jesus is Lord' were the earliest Christian creed and were therefore of the greatest possible importance to the early church. From the earliest days it was recognised that if a person confessed 'Jesus is Lord,' he or she was to be received for baptism. This is because, on the one hand, 'No one can say, "Jesus is Lord," except by the Holy Spirit' (1 Cor. 12:3) and because, on the other hand, 'If you confess with your mouth, "Jesus is Lord," and believe in your heart that God raised him from the dead, you will be saved' (Rom. 10:9). To us, who read these records at a later date, it seems strange that 'Jesus is Lord' could be so important to our spiritual predecessors, but the reason is that these words literally overflow with meaning.

To say that Jesus is Lord implies two things. First, it implies that Jesus is God, the point of the angel's announcement. Secondly, it implies that Jesus is the Saviour.

The first of these implications is due to the fact that in the Greek version of the Old Testament (the Septuagint), which was well known to the Jewish community of the first century and from which most of the New Testament writers quoted when citing Scripture, *kyrios* (Lord) is used to translate the great Hebrew name for God: *Yahweh* or *Jehovah*. This is why most of our English Bibles do not use the name *Yahweh* but have Lord instead.

The disciples of Christ knew that this word was repeatedly used to translate this great name for God. Yet, knowing this, they did not hesitate to transfer the title to Jesus, thereby indicating that in their view Jesus is Jehovah.

We need to be careful at this point, of course, because not all uses of the word 'Lord' in the New Testament imply divinity. 'Lord' was a bit like our English word 'sir'. On the most common level it could be used merely as a form of polite address. That is why, according to the Gospels, apparent unbelievers sometimes called Jesus 'Lord'. This does not mean that they had received a sudden revelation of who he was but only that they were treating him with the respect due to a distinguished rabbi. They were being polite. On the other hand, 'Lord' could mean more. When we speak of Sir Winston Churchill we are using our word 'sir' as a title. Similarly, those who called Jesus 'Lord' were sometimes confessing that he was their 'Master' by this greeting. In the most exalted instances, as in Thomas' great confession, 'My Lord and my God' (John 20:28), the word was linked to the disciples' belief in Christ's divinity.

This is the meaning of *kyrios* in the great Christological passages of the New Testament. Here are some examples.

(1) *First Corinthians 8:4-6*. 'We know that an idol is nothing at all in the world and that there is no God but one. For even if there are so-called gods, whether in heaven or on earth (as indeed there are many "gods" and many "lords"), yet for us there is but one God, the Father, from whom all things came and for whom we live; and there is but one Lord, Jesus Christ, through whom all things came and through whom we live.' The background for

this passage is the polytheism of the Greek world, which Paul is refuting. He is arguing that there is but one God, who is one with Jesus. The parallelism between 'from whom all things came and for whom we live' (applied to God the Father) and 'through whom all things came and through whom we live' (applied to Jesus Christ) makes this identification plain.

(2) *Psalm 110:1*. On one occasion, recorded in Matthew 22:41-46, Jesus asked his enemies who they thought the Christ was to be. They replied, 'The son of David.' This was true as far as it went; but they were thinking of an earthly, human Messiah, and Jesus wanted them to see further. So he referred them to this Old Testament text, asking,

> 'How is it then that David, speaking by the Spirit, calls him "Lord"? For he says,
>
> > "The Lord said to my Lord:
> > 'Sit at my right hand
> > until I put your enemies
> > under your feet.'"
>
> If then David calls him "Lord", how can he be his son?' (vv. 43-45).

Jesus' point was that if David called the Messiah 'Lord,' it could only be because the Messiah was to be more than just one of his descendants. He would have to be a divine Messiah, which is what the title 'Lord' indicates.

Peter had this text in mind when he told the Sanhedrin, 'God has exalted him [Jesus] to his own right hand as Prince and Saviour' (Acts 5:31).

Paul was thinking of these words when he wrote, 'Since, then, you have been raised with Christ, set your hearts on things above, where Christ is seated at the right hand of God' (Col. 3:1).

The author of Hebrews used the text early in his letter (and also at two later points), writing that Jesus, 'after he had provided purification for our sins ... sat down at the right hand of the Majesty in heaven' (Heb. 1:3; cf. 8:1 and 12:2).

(3) *Philippians 2:5-11*. The great Christological hymn of Philippians 2 is the clearest text of all.

> Your attitude should be the same as that of Christ Jesus:
> Who, being in very nature God,
> did not consider equality with God
> something to be grasped,
> but made himself nothing,
> taking the very nature of a servant,
> being made in human likeness.
> And being found in appearance as a man,
> he humbled himself
> and became obedient to death –
> even death on a cross!
> Therefore God exalted him to the highest place
> and gave him the name that is above every name,
> that at the name of Jesus every knee should bow,
> in heaven and on earth and under the earth,
> and every tongue confess that Jesus Christ is Lord,
> to the glory of God the Father.

What is the 'name that is above every name'? It is not the name Jesus itself, though the wording seems to suggest this to the English reader. It is the name 'Lord'; for that is God's own name, and no name can be higher.

The meaning of this title shows why the early Christians would not apply the word 'Lord' to any other. If they had done so, they would have repudiated Christ. One famous case is that of the aged Bishop of Smyrna, Polycarp, who was martyred on February 22, AD 156. As he was driven to the arena two of the city officials, who had respect for him because of his age and reputation, tried to persuade him to comply with the demand to honour Caesar. 'What harm is there in saying, "Caesar is Lord," and burning incense ... and saving yourself?' they asked. Polycarp refused. Later, in the arena, he explained his position, saying, 'For eighty-six years I have been [Christ's] slave, and he has done me no wrong; how can I blaspheme my King who saved me?' Polycarp refused to call Caesar Lord, because 'Lord' meant 'God' and there can only be one God. If Polycarp had called Caesar Lord, then Jesus could not have been Lord for Polycarp and Polycarp could not have been a Christian.

Those who recorded Polycarp's story shared his convictions, for they concluded the account by saying: 'He [Polycarp] was arrested by Herod, when Philip of Tralles was high priest, and Statius Quadratus was governor, *but our Lord Jesus Christ was reigning for ever*. To him be glory, honour, majesty and eternal dominion from generation to generation. Amen.'[2]

Lord and Saviour

The second implication of the title Lord is that Jesus is the Saviour. This is linked to his lordship because, as John R. W. Stott writes,

> The title 'Lord' is a symbol of Christ's victory over the forces of evil. If Jesus has been exalted over all the principalities and powers of evil, as indeed he has, this is the reason why he has been called Lord. If Jesus has been proclaimed Lord, as he has, it is because these powers are under his feet. He has conquered them on the cross, and therefore our salvation – that is to say,

---

[2] 'The Martyrdom of Holy Polycarp, Bishop of Smyrna' in *The Apostolic Fathers: An American Translation*, trans. by Edgar J. Goodspeed (New York: Harper & Brothers, 1950) pp. 250, 251, 255.

our rescue from sin, Satan, fear and death – is due to
that victory.[3]

In recent years it has become customary in some parts of
the evangelical world to distinguish between the lordship
and saviourhood of Christ in such a way that one is supposed to be able to have Jesus as Saviour without having
him as Lord. It is argued that requiring Christ to be Lord in
the matter of salvation means adding commitment to faith
and that this is a false and accursed gospel (Gal. 1:6-9).

There are two serious mistakes at this point. One involves the meaning of faith. Is 'faith' minus commitment
true biblical faith? Hardly! Biblical faith involves three elements: (1) knowledge, upon which it is based; (2) heart
response, which results from the new birth; and (3) commitment, without which 'faith' is no different from the
assent of the demons who only 'believe ... and shudder'
(James 2:19). Faith without commitment is not true faith.
It is a 'dead' faith which will save no one.

The second mistake is even more serious, because it
involves the person and work of Jesus himself. Who is
this one who has saved us from our sins? He is, as Paul
has it, 'Jesus Christ our Lord'. No true Christian will add
anything to the finished work of Jesus. To do so really is
to proclaim a false gospel. We direct people to the Lord
Jesus Christ. Nevertheless, he is the Lord Jesus Christ.
This Lord is the object of faith and its content. There is
no other. Consequently, if faith is directed to one who is
not Lord, it is directed to one who is a false Christ of the
imagination. Such a one is not the Saviour, and he will
save no one.[4]

---

[3] John R. W. Stott, 'The Sovereignty of God the Son' in *Our Sovereign God:
Addresses Presented to the Philadelphia Conference on Reformed Theology 1974–
1976*, ed. by James M. Boice (Grand Rapids: Baker Book House, 1977), p. 18

[4] For a fuller discussion of these arguments see James Montgomery Boice,
Christ's Call to Discipleship (Chicago: Moody Press, 1986), pp. 19-21.

Is He The Lord?

At this point it is easy to sit back and congratulate ourselves on having a sound theology. Of course, we know that Jesus must be Lord to be Saviour. Of course, we know that true faith involves commitment. But is Jesus really our Lord? Are we truly committed to him? In the study of Christ's lordship by John Stott, from which I quoted earlier, six implications are suggested.

(1) *An intellectual implication.* If Jesus is our Lord, then he must be Lord of our thinking. He must be Lord of our minds. On one occasion, when the Lord called disciples, he said, 'Take my yoke upon you and learn from me' (Matt. 11:29), meaning that he was to be the disciples' teacher. He is our teacher today.

How does Jesus do this, seeing that he is not with us physically as he was in the time of the disciples? The answer is that he teaches us through Scripture. That is why we must be men and women of the Book – if we truly are Christ's followers. Left to ourselves, we will stray into many kinds of false thinking – just as the world does. But if we regularly read and study the Bible, asking the Holy Spirit to interpret it to us, and then try to live out what we understand, we will increasingly come to think as Christ thinks and discover that we have an entirely new outlook on the world. We will see people from God's perspective, and we will not be taken in by the world's false ideas.

(2) *An ethical implication.* In the study I referred to earlier, Stott points out that Jesus is not just Lord of our minds. He is Lord of our wills and of our moral standards too.

> It is not only what we believe that is to come under the lordship of Jesus but also how we behave. Discipleship implies obedience, and obedience implies that there are absolute moral commands that we are required

to obey. To refer to Jesus politely as 'our Lord' is not enough. He still says to us, 'Why do you call me Lord and do not the things that I say?' In today's miasma of relativity we need to maintain unashamedly the absolute moral standards of the Lord. Further, we need to go on and teach that the yoke of Jesus is easy and his burden is light, and that under the yoke of Jesus we have not bondage but freedom and rest.[5]

(3) *A vocational implication.* If Jesus is Lord, then he is not only Lord of our minds, wills and morals. He is Lord of our time; and this means that he is Lord of our professions, jobs, careers and ambitions. We cannot plan our lives as if our relationship to Jesus is somehow detached from those plans and irrelevant to them.

Paul is an example at this point. Before he met Christ on the road to Damascus and bowed before him, Paul was pursuing a vocation of his own choice. He was a Pharisee intent on rising high in the intellectual and ruling structures of Judaism. He knew where he was going. When he met Jesus all this was redirected. The first words Jesus uttered after he had stopped Paul in his tracks by asking, 'Saul, Saul, why do you persecute me?' (Acts 9:4) and by identifying himself as Jesus, were: 'Get up and go into the city, and you will be told what you must do' (v. 6). Paul obeyed Jesus and was told what he was to do. He was to be Christ's apostle to the Gentiles. Later, when he gave a defence of his activities before King Agrippa, he quoted the Lord as saying to him, 'I have appeared to you to appoint you as a servant and as a witness of what you have seen of me and what I will show you. I will rescue you from your own people and from the Gentiles. I am sending you to them to open their eyes and turn them from darkness to light, and from the power of Satan

---

[5] John R. W. Stott, 'The Sovereignty of God the Son,' p. 22

133

to God' (Acts 26:16-18). He concluded, 'So then, King Agrippa, I was not disobedient to the vision' (v. 19).

This is precisely the way we must regard our vocations. We are not called to be apostles, as Paul was. Only a few are called even to what we designate religious work. But whether we work in a church or a factory, in a hospital, a law firm or a small business, whether we are homemakers or builders of homes – whatever our calling, we must regard it as a form of Christian service and know that we are obeying the Lord Jesus Christ as we pursue it.

(4) *An ecclesiastical implication*. Jesus is also head of the church. This truth delivers us from two banes. One is disorder. It occurs when those who are members of the church pursue their own course, including what they wish their church to be – without regard to the guidelines for church life laid down in the Bible or without proper consideration for those who are their brothers and sisters in the Lord. The second is clericalism. It occurs when lay people abandon their God-given role in the church, or when pastors tyrannise the church without acknowledging that they are servants of the people as well as servants of Christ and that they must serve the church as Jesus served it.

(5) *A political implication*. Today, when we talk about the lordship of Christ, we face a battle on two fronts. One is an intra-mural battle. It is a battle that goes on within the Christian fellowship. It is the battle I was speaking about earlier when I opposed attempts to separate the saving work of Christ from his lordship.

But there is another battle also. It is extra-mural. That is, it goes on outside the church's fellowship. It comes from those who, in a certain sense, may be quite tolerant of religion but who insist that religion must be kept in its place – 'on the reservation' – and that, above all, it must not intrude into our national life. We are fighting this battle today. And we are saying – at least I hope so – that Jesus is not only our own personal Lord, not only Lord of the church which he founded; he is also Lord of all life, the life of nations included. He is not merely our King; he is the King of kings. He is not merely our Lord; he is the Lord of lords. Therefore, we who are Christians stand as his representatives in history to call this world to account. We are here to remind the world that this same Jesus Christ whom we serve has spoken from heaven to reveal what true righteousness is, both for individuals and nations, and that those who disregard him do so at their own peril and must one day give an account.

Yet this must be done rightly. First, it must be done humbly. For we are not perfect – we too must appear before Jesus – and those to whom we speak are ultimately answerable to him and not to us. Secondly, we must know that our mission is to be by example and word, not by force. Otherwise we will become triumphalists. We must remember that the Lord did not come to set up an army or even a political party but rather a witnessing fellowship, and that when the church has departed from the Lord's pattern in this area, it has always done so to its harm.

(6) *A global implication.* The final implication flows from the Great Commission in which, on the basis of his own authority, the Lord sent disciples into the entire world to make and disciple Christians everywhere (Matt. 28:18-20). The lordship of Jesus is the most powerful of missionary incentives. It is as Lord of our lives that he tells us to go, and because we know him as Lord this is exactly what we do. Because we love him we want everyone to become his disciple.

I close with the questions I asked at the beginning of this list of implications. Is Jesus your Lord? Are you truly committed to him? If you are, your life can never be what it would be otherwise. You can be certain that the shepherds bowed before the message of the angels. You should also bow before him of whom the angels spoke.

11

JOY TO YOU AND ME

(Luke 2:10)

> But the angel said to them, 'Do not be afraid. I bring you good news of great joy that will be for all the people.'

There are many emotions associated with observing Christmas, but there is no emotion so characteristic of Christmas as joy. The whole atmosphere of Christmas is joyful, and it has been so ever since the angels announced the birth of Jesus to the shepherds in the fields around Bethlehem. That is why we sing about joy so often in our carols:

> O come, all ye faithful,
> Joyful and triumphant....
>
> Dear desire of every nation,
> Joy of every longing heart.
>
> Joyful, all ye nations rise,
> Join the triumph of the skies.
>
> And best of all ...
> Joy to the world! The Lord is come....

What is joy? The dictionary defines joy as 'a vivid emotion of pleasure arising from a sense of well-being or satisfaction, the feeling or state of being highly pleased or delighted' (*Oxford English Dictionary*). But that is not a very satisfactory definition. It seems so ... well, joyless. The reason joy is so hard to define is that it seems to stand alone, there being nothing quite like it. This is probably why C. S. Lewis entitled his brilliant autobiography *Surprised by Joy*. He was surprised by joy, because he had never known anything like joy until he found it in Jesus Christ.

Usually we can define something by reference to its opposite. But what is the opposite of joy? It is not sorrow really, though the marriage service links the two as contrary human experiences: 'in joy or in sorrow'. (A better opposite to sorrow is happiness.) Nor is joy the exact opposite of melancholy or pain or disappointment or grief or unhappiness.

Joy is its own unique emotion. And the clear reason for this is that it has its source in the character of the unique and altogether 'different' God.

The First Christmas
We find joy throughout the Christmas story, in the experience of the story's main characters.

(1) *The Angels*. The best-known statement of joy is the utterance of the angels to the shepherds: 'Do not be afraid. I bring you good news of great joy that will be for all the people.' But those who announced joy to the shepherds had themselves first experienced it, which was why they were singing praises to God in the night skies above Bethlehem. And why should they not have been singing? The Lord Jesus Christ later told us that the angels rejoice in heaven over even one sinner who repents (Luke 15:7, 10).

So how could they not rejoice over the birth of him who was to save not only a solitary sinner, but many?

The rejoicing of the angels tells us that there was *heavenly* joy at the birth of Jesus.

(2) *The Shepherds*. The shepherds also rejoiced. If the rejoicing of the angels was a heavenly joy, theirs was clearly an *earthly* and very *humble* joy. They might have missed this joy in a variety of ways, thinking perhaps that the angels' 'good news' was for others more important or better instructed than themselves, a mistake many people make today. But they did not make this mistake. Instead of dismissing the message as intended for people other than themselves, they hurried to Bethlehem, saw the baby, and then returned to their sheep 'glorifying and praising God for all the things they had heard and seen, which were just as they had been told' (v. 20).

One of the things they had been told is that they would find the baby 'wrapped in cloths and lying in a manger' (v. 12), and perhaps this simple circumstance was a major reason for their joy. If the Saviour had been born in a palace, these men would have been turned away at the door. They would equally have been denied access to the halls of the high priest or other leaders in Jerusalem, or to the castle of Herod. They might even have been turned away by the innkeeper, as Mary and Joseph had been. Jesus had not been born in any of these finer places. He had been born where any person could come to him, however humble their circumstances or disadvantaged their life or education.

That is still true today, and it is still a reason for joy. Jesus is accessible. You do not have to be important in the world's eyes or be highly educated or rich or anything else to come to him.

(3) *Mary*. The shepherds were filled with joy, but I am sure this did not hinder them from noticing the joy of Jesus' mother, Mary. For hers must have been a very great joy indeed. At one point the Bible speaks of the pain of childbirth, saying, 'A woman giving birth to a child has pain because her time has come; but when her baby is born she forgets the anguish because of her joy that a child is born into the world' (John 16:21). If this is true of the birth of nearly any child, as it undoubtedly is, how much greater must the joy of Mary have been when she gave birth to the One she knew would be the Saviour? Mary's joy was a *profound* joy, for she was a deep and godly woman. The Bible says that in her joy Mary 'treasured up all these things and pondered them in her heart' (v. 19).

(4) *Joseph*. What about Joseph? Joseph tends to be the forgotten person in the Christmas story, attention generally being riveted upon the child and his mother. But Joseph must have been overcome with joy too. His would have been an *awesome* joy, for an angel had appeared to him months before to explain Mary's conception as something unique and supernatural: 'Joseph son of David, do not be afraid to take Mary home as your wife, because what is conceived in her is from the Holy Spirit. She will give birth to a son, and you are to give him the name Jesus, because he will save his people from their sins' (Matt. 1:20, 21). Joseph, no less than Mary, must have said to the angel, 'May it be to me as you have said' (Luke 1:38).

(5) *The Wise Men*. The last people to come upon the scene are the Wise Men, whom most of our modern versions call Magi. They came from the east, asking when they arrived in Jerusalem, 'Where is the one who has been born king of the Jews? We saw his star in the east and have come to worship him' (Matt. 2:2). Nobody knew what they were

talking about, of course. But after Herod had consulted with the teachers of the law and the prophecy of Micah had been recalled by them – 'But you, Bethlehem, in the land of Judah, are by no means least among the rulers of Judah; for out of you will come a ruler who will be the shepherd of my people Israel' (v. 6) – the Wise Men went to Bethlehem and, led by the star they had been following earlier, found Jesus. The text says, 'When they saw the star they were overjoyed' and that when they found the young child they 'worshipped him ... and presented him with gifts of gold and of incense and of myrrh' (vv. 10, 11).

The joy of the Wise Men was *extravagant*. Intellectuals, which is what these Magi were, are not supposed to be extravagant in their actions. They are supposed to be calm, balanced and deliberate. But these men did not hesitate from expressing the joy that was bursting from their excited minds and hearts. This was the world's Saviour – their Saviour. So they expressed their joy accordingly.

Isn't it interesting that the birth of Jesus was witnessed, on the one hand, by shepherds – the least of all the lowly people of that day – and, on the other hand, by Wise Men, who were among the world's most important persons? This tells us that the gospel is for everybody. The angel's announcement to the shepherds disproves the thought that the gospel is too exalted for the common or disadvantaged person, while the coming of the Wise Men disproves the thought that the gospel is too simple for the rich or prominent person or the distinguished intellectual.

Joy For All People

This brings me to the next important observation on our text, the most important thing of all from our perspective. The text says, 'Do not be afraid. I bring you good news of great joy that will be *for all the people*.' Have you ever thought about that explicitly before? The joy the angel was announcing was not to be confined to a select few – the shepherds or Mary or Joseph or the wise men, for example. It was for 'all the people'. And while it is true that in the context of the Jewish community of the first century those words probably meant 'for all the *Jewish* people,' we know from later portions of the story that all the peoples of the world, Gentiles as well as Jews, were embraced by the announcement.

After the birth of the child, when his parents brought him to Jerusalem to present him to the Lord, according to Exodus 13:2, 12, aged Simeon appeared, took Jesus in his arms and praised God, calling the child,

> 'a light for revelation *to the Gentiles*
> and for glory to your people Israel' (Luke 2:32).

This stands at the beginning of the story. Later on, at the end, we find the same emphasis. We find Jesus speaking to his disciples, giving them a command for world evangelism. He says, 'All authority in heaven and on earth has been given to me. Therefore go and make disciples of all nations, baptising them in the name of the Father and of the Son and of the Holy Spirit, and teaching them to obey everything I have commanded you. And surely I am with you always, to the very end of the age' (Matt. 28:18-20).

From the beginning to the end it was recognised that the 'good news of great joy' was not to be restricted to one people or one race but was for everybody.

It is for me.

It is for you, if you will come to Jesus.

Our Joy is Jesus

The next point of this message, which I have already suggested, is the most obvious. But it is also the point which most needs to be stressed. It is true that the joy of

Christmas is for everybody – for Jew and Gentile, high and low, educated and uneducated, sophisticated and simple – but this does not mean that the joy of Christmas is everybody's, even less that it can be found in any place at all. This joy is the joy of Christmas, and this means that it is bound to and is utterly inseparable from Jesus Christ.

One of the great Bible dictionaries, *Hastings' Dictionary of the Bible*, points out that 'a striking point of similarity between Old Testament and New Testament piety is that, in both cases, God himself is the object and ground of the believer's joy.'[1] The article cites such texts as: Psalm 35:9 ('Then my soul will rejoice in the LORD and delight in his salvation'), Psalm 43:4 ('Then will I go to the altar of God, to God, my joy and my delight') and Philippians 3:1 ('Finally, my brothers, rejoice in the Lord!'). But it also points out, through a variety of texts, that the Old Testament experience is sharpened and focused by the coming of Jesus, which is only what we should expect. A typical New Testament expression is found in Romans 5:11, '...we also rejoice in God through our Lord Jesus Christ, through whom we have now received reconciliation.'

Joy is focused in Christ, because Christ has achieved our salvation. Joy is intensified in Christ, because he has accomplished what, in Old Testament times, was only anticipated.

Joy of the Gospel
William Barclay, the well-known Scottish preacher and teacher, has a study of joy in which he stresses its importance throughout the New Testament. In the New Testament the verb *chairein*, which means 'to rejoice,' occurs 72 times, and the word *chara*, which means 'joy,'

---

[1] James Hastings, *A Dictionary of the Bible* (New York: Charles Scribner's & Sons, 1958), vol. 2, p. 790.

occurs 60 times. Because of Jesus the New Testament is a book of great joy. Here are the points with which Barclay supports his observations:

(1) *Joy is the distinguishing atmosphere of the Christian life.* 'Rejoice in the Lord always. I will say it again: Rejoice!' Paul writes to his friends at Philippi. Whatever comes into our lives – whether pain or pleasure, good times or bad – we can be joyful. Here joy is most clearly distinguished from happiness, which is the world's equivalent virtue. Secular people can be happy, if the circumstances are right. This is because 'happiness' is built upon the word *happenstance*, which refers to circumstances. If the happenings of life just happen to be right, the person is happy. If they are wrong, he is not. Joy is not like that. Joy is not grounded in circumstances; joy is grounded in God. Consequently, the true Christian can be joyful whatever circumstances may come into his or her life.

Barclay says, 'There is no virtue in the Christian life which is not made radiant with joy; there is no circumstance and no occasion which is not illumined with joy. A joyless life is not a Christian life, for joy is the one constant in the recipe for Christian living.'[2]

(2) *There is joy in Christian fellowship.* I notice in the Christmas story that none of the main characters ever appear in isolation. At the heart of the story there are three: Mary, Joseph and the baby. The shepherds are presented as a group of individuals, at least two and no doubt more. So also with the Wise Men. Even the angels are 'a great company,' a 'host'.

This is no accident. Barclay says, 'In the New Testament there is nothing of that religion so-called which isolates

---

[2] William Barclay, *Flesh and Spirit: An Examination of Galatians 5:19-23* (Nashville: Abingdon Press, 1962), p. 78.

a man from his fellow-men. The New Testament vividly knows the joy of making friends and keeping friends and reuniting friends, for friendship and reconciliation between man and man are the reflection of fellowship and reconciliation between man and God.'[3] The greatest of all possible supports for evangelism is the sight of true Christian fellowship, what the Bible calls 'joy in the Lord'. And, by contrast, the greatest hindrance to the sharing of the gospel is the sight of a church in which that fellowship has been lost, neglected or destroyed.

(3) *There is joy in the gospel.* All I have been saying leads to this point. Joy is seen at the beginning of the gospel, at the time of Christ's birth ('good news of great joy'). It is seen also at the end, when the angels again appear, telling the women who have come to the tomb of Jesus, 'Do not be afraid, for I know that you are looking for Jesus, who was crucified. He is not here; he has risen, just as he said. Come and see the place where he lay' (Matt. 28:5, 6). We are told that after the women had done this 'they hurried away from the tomb, afraid yet filled with joy' (v. 8). After this, after Jesus had appeared to the disciples and then had ascended to heaven, we are told that the disciples 'returned to Jerusalem with great joy' (Luke 24:52).

Barclay points out that there is joy in 'receiving' the gospel (cf. Luke 19:6; Acts 8:8, 39; 1 Thess. 1:6). There is joy in 'believing' the gospel also (Rom. 15:13).

(4) *Christian work and witness is a source of joy for Christians.* Why? Because God works when Christians speak or work for him, and nothing in life is quite as thrilling as seeing God work. I would add that there is a special joy in 'preaching' the gospel, because nothing so thrills the heart of a true believer as making Christ so clearly known

---

[3] *Ibid.*, p. 79

145

to another that the other person believes on him also and becomes a Christian.

In the Reformed tradition much is made of the need to awaken sorrow and guilt, to 'slay' the hearer by the law in order that he may be 'raised' by the gospel, as it is sometimes expressed. I am willing to admit that there is truth in that. I have even been accused of preaching nothing but a 'fire and brimstone' gospel myself. But let me say this: 'fire and brimstone' may awaken a sinner to his need of the gospel, but wrath does not save anyone. It is the message of joy in the work of Jesus Christ that saves men and women. Repentance? Yes. Repentance is indispensable. But after repentance there must be faith in the gospel of grace and joy in the assurance that the believing one has been forgiven by God for his sin.

The great missionary E. Stanley Jones used to tell of a man named Rufus Moseley, whom he called 'the most bubbling Christian' he ever knew. Someone once said of Moseley, 'The first time I heard him I thought he was crazy. The second time I heard him I knew he was crazy.' Moseley was so filled with joy that he just couldn't keep quiet or settle down. Someone, who wanted to sober him up, once asked Moseley if he thought Jesus had ever laughed. (There is no record in the Bible that he did.) Moseley said, 'I don't know. But he fixed me up so I can laugh.'[4]

Shouldn't that be the testimony of all Christians?

A Joyful Christmas

So let's laugh this Christmas. Let's be joyful.

Gather your friends around and talk of God's great blessings. Remember the past. Tell your children how God has cared for you, even in hard and difficult times. And if you are going through hard times now, as many

---

[4] Barclay tells this story on p. 82.

are, remember that you can be joyful even in the midst of such circumstances.

The Christmas 1987 issue of *The War Cry*, the promotional magazine of The Salvation Army, contains an article on 'Joy at Christmas' in which the author tells this story. At the time the most expensive perfume in the world was called Joy, and she knew of a woman who had been sent a bottle in the mail. Unfortunately, the package was crushed in the post, and all that arrived was faintly-scented wrapping paper. Joy had disappeared![5]

The joy that fills our lives when we have come to Christ does not evaporate. It is always present, and it transforms everything.

I do not know whether it is proper to ascribe feelings of joy to the rest of God's creation – to animals, who do not have souls and therefore do not fellowship with God, in addition to men and women, who alone can understand the gospel. But Peter, Paul and Mary did it when they sang,

> Joy to the fishes in the deep blue sea,
> And joy to you and me.

That may not be entirely right, as I have indicated. But there is something right about it. The joy of Christmas is not for people of a bygone age, not for people other than ourselves. It is for 'you and me' if we will have it.

Will you have it?

The first of all Christmas sermons, the sermon of the angels, proclaimed 'good news of great joy ... for all the people.'

What is that good news of great joy?

> 'Today in the town of David a Saviour has been born to you: he is Christ the Lord.'

---

[5] Eva Barrows, 'Joy at Christmas,' *The War Cry*, Christmas 1987, p. 2

12

'Come to Bethlehem'

(Luke 2:15-18)

When the angels had left them and gone into heaven, the shepherds said to one another, 'Let's go to Bethlehem and see this thing that has happened, which the Lord has told us about.'

So they hurried off and found Mary and Joseph, and the baby, who was lying in the manger. When they had seen him, they spread the word concerning what had been told them about this child, and all who heard it were amazed at what the shepherds said to them.

At Christmas we often speak of the annunciation. When we use that word, we are usually thinking about the angel's announcement to Mary that she would conceive and bear a son and that her son would be Jesus, the Saviour of the world. But strictly speaking, that is not the only annunciation in the story. There was an annunciation to Joseph, recorded in Matthew 1. And in the great story with which we are most familiar, the story recorded in Luke 2, there is a further annunciation to shepherds who were out in the fields surrounding Bethlehem. The angel who appeared to them announced that Jesus had been born in David's city and that they would find him lying in a manger.

Those were the three angelic announcements. But we could add to those annunciations the fact that later there were human annunciations to other people. The shepherds especially announced these things to others, because we are told in the story that they told everyone 'what had been told them about this child' (Luke 2:17).

The text I would like to look at in this study is one that occurs between the two annunciations involving the shepherds: the annunciation of the angels to them and their annunciation to other people. In between these two announcements there is an invitation the shepherds gave to one another. We are not told exactly who said it. But after the angels had left and gone into heaven, we are told that they said to one another, 'Let's go to Bethlehem and see this thing that has happened, which the Lord has told us about' (v. 15). The angels had not commanded them. They did not say, 'Go to Bethlehem,' but that was certainly the tenor of their announcement. So the shepherds said, 'Well then, let's go and see what we have been told about.'

I want to reflect on that.

An Important Journey

There are all kinds of journeys that people make at Christmas. When I talk to people in church on the Sunday before Christmas, church members will introduce me to relatives who are visiting. Often it is in the context of a journey. They have come from the west coast to be in Philadelphia for the holidays, or from some other place. Or sometimes people say to me, 'I wish I could be here next Sunday, but I have to go home to be with my parents.' There is always a great deal of travel at this season.

I suppose that of all the Christmas journeys there have been, there has never been a journey as significant as the one the shepherds took from the fields surrounding Bethlehem, where they were watching their sheep, into the city of David to see Jesus on that first Christmas evening.

The shepherds were going into the city to see the baby, and on their way they passed through the city. I would like to think that they were thoughtful men. So they might have given some thought to the kind of city they were passing through.

(1) *A sinful city*. They would have seen it as a sinful city, first of all, just as our cities are. A sinful city, in a sinful country, in a sinful world, filled with sinful people – because that's the way the world is. It always has been, ever since the fall of Adam and Eve in Eden. Of all the things we can say about humanity, the most significant from a spiritual point of view is that we are sinful human beings. We were not made that way. We were made in perfect fellowship and communion with God. But we have rebelled against God's commands, saying, 'I do not want to abide by God's commands, because if I do, it means that I will not be in sovereign control of my life, and I want to have control.' So we take our lives into our own hands and lose them by doing so.

All through human history the thing that has most tied the human race together is its sin. It makes no difference whether we come from the white race or the black race, whether we are Americans or Europeans, from North America or South America, rich or poor. Whoever we are and wherever we come from, our rebellion against God is the most important thing that ties us together as human beings. So those who lay asleep in Bethlehem that night (or perhaps were even awake that night and up to some mischief) were sinful people.

We do not know a lot about this city, so it is hard to be specific about Bethlehem's sins. Bethlehem was not the kind of city about which people were writing books. Even

Jerusalem was not that kind of city. Still we get a glimpse of Bethlehem's sins from the teachings of Jesus Christ. When he grew to manhood he began to travel around the country teaching people about the kingdom of God, sometimes in stories.

One story was about a prodigal son. It was a story everyone would have understood. They knew what it was to have families divided against families, to have children who disobey and run away. When Jesus told this story there would have been a confirming echo in the hearts of many who were listening.

He also told a story about an unjust judge. The judge was supposed to apply the law impartially. Yet when a poor widow came and had no money to pay him, he didn't want to bother with her case at all. In the end, he finally did what she wanted, but only because she was pestering him. When Jesus told that story the people of his day would have understood exactly what such legal injustices were like. They knew of sinful magistrates, because theirs was a sinful world.

Again, Jesus told stories about people who were entrusted with other people's property. In one such story there were stewards who were supposed to manage the land and then, when harvest time came, render an honest account to the owner. But the stewards did not do that. They conspired to keep the profits for themselves. And when the owner sent servants to receive what he was owed, the stewards beat the servants and in the end even killed one. When Jesus talked in such terms he was describing a world everyone understood.

Bethlehem was filled with such people, just like other cities. In fact, Bethlehem was filled with the kind of people who one day were going to become incensed with Jesus Christ and conspire to get rid of him. They would say, 'We will not have this man around here any more. We can't have his kind in our world. We have to get rid of people like this.' So eventually they managed to get him crucified, though he was completely innocent and was even declared to be so by Pilate. That is what Bethlehem was like.

That is what our cities are like too – sinful cities. You do not even have to be particularly well informed or sensitive to notice it. My church is in the middle of the city, and I notice that sometimes, even on a Sunday morning or evening, we will be in church and hear police cars going by outside, their sirens sounding. We know that something is wrong. Perhaps it's a robbery, a mugging. Perhaps a shooting. We go home at night, turn on the television and hear about it. That is the kind of city the shepherds had to pass through on the way to see Jesus.

(2) *A calloused city*. To carry this line of thought a bit further, we might also observe that Bethlehem was a calloused city, a hard city. And that follows, doesn't it? One thing sin does is harden the heart. So if Bethlehem was sinful, it follows that it would be calloused, and it was.

We know that Bethlehem, in particular, was calloused because we have been told the circumstances that surrounded the birth of Jesus. Here were two poor people from Nazareth, Joseph and Mary, and Mary was expecting a child. They had travelled the long distance to Bethlehem because Caesar Augustus had ordered a census, and everybody had to go to his home city. Joseph was from Bethlehem. So, although they lived in Nazareth, to Bethlehem they had to go. Travel must have been difficult for Mary. And to make matters worse, when they got to Bethlehem there was no room for them, not even for one in her condition. Probably the rich would have found a place. The rich had friends, and the rich will always take the rich in. But this poor couple had nowhere to stay, and no one would share their accommodation. When they finally did find refuge it was in a stable. Tradition says it was a cave. It was there, among the animals, that Mary gave birth to Jesus and placed him in a manger.

Our cities are like that too. If you are a person of means or have influence, you can get around in the city and do all right. But if you do not have these things, the city is a hard, hard place. People do not have room for you. 'You can't stay here. Go somewhere else. Someone else will take care of you. But not us. Not here. Not now,' they tell you.

(3) *A divided city.* Bethlehem was a divided city too. There were all kinds of divisions – rich against poor, race against race. The Jews were divided against the Samaritans. Being a captive nation, under the heel of the Romans, the Jews, together with the Samaritans and the other oppressed people of the east, hated this powerful authoritarian force.

One year just before Christmas I received a form letter from astronaut Bud Nelson, who has been a representative to Congress from the eleventh district in Florida. He told of the time when he was circling the earth in the spacecraft *Columbia.* At one point he looked out of a window at night and could see in one glance the whole eastern coast of the Mediterranean, all the way from the headwaters of the Nile in the south, north, extending almost into Russia. He could see the lights of all the cities and towns of that region – Cairo and Alexandria in Egypt, Jerusalem and Tel Aviv in Israel, Amman in Jordan, and so on. It looked so beautiful at night, so wonderful. But he said in that letter that the sight caused him to reflect on the tensions that had torn that one limited area of the world for centuries and were, in fact, going on at that very moment. People were killing each other. Races were hating other races, as one nation, culture or language was fiercely divided from another.

(4) *A sad city*. Bethlehem was a sad city, too. If you study the documents that have survived from the ancient world, one thing you will be impressed with, if you think along these lines, is that it was not a happy time. It was a sad time. It was sad for all the nations. Greece had passed its glory. There had been a day when the Greek philosophers had lifted Greece to the pinnacle of influence, but that day was gone. Nobody was paying much attention to philosophy. Greece had waned. Rome was the dominant power in the world, but it was already starting to decline. The Roman republic had disappeared. It was only a matter of time before the Roman Empire would fall.

Judea was a captive land dominated politically by Rome and oppressed by its own spiritual leaders who were as cruel as the Romans, and self-righteous too. People had no joy. Joy had gone out of their lives, and they were merely scraping along – many of them desperately poor, struggling just to survive from day to day. If they had known the words, they might have recited Macbeth's speech from Shakespeare's play:

> Tomorrow, and tomorrow, and tomorrow
> Creeps in this petty pace from day to day,
> To the last syllable of recorded time;
> And all our yesterdays have lighted fools
> The way to dusty death.

What a sinful, calloused, divided, dismal world it was to which Christ came! Of course, I do not know for certain whether the shepherds thought of all these things as they passed through the city of Bethlehem that night, but they may have. At any rate, they had experienced these things personally.

We See Jesus

But what did they find when they got to the manger? They found Jesus, of course. They found the baby lying in a manger, wrapped in cloths, as the angel had said. But what they found in Jesus was one who was in himself an amazing, marvellous, overwhelming contrast to everything they had seen about them in the world as they had passed through Bethlehem.

(1) *Purity instead of sin.* They had passed through a very sinful city, but when they found Jesus they found one who was not in the least sinful. Indeed, they found the very essence of purity. A baby always seems pure anyway. We see a newborn child and say, 'Oh, look at the innocent babe. How beautiful.' Yet when we talk about human children we are, nevertheless, talking about children who are sinful. We carry the germ of sin within us, even as infants. That is why children are so selfish and show it so early. Very soon they learn to lie and steal and do other wrong things. But in this case the shepherds came to one who was not merely an outward picture of purity or a symbol of purity, as other infants are, but was purity itself.

Jesus is the one in whom no sin was found. As he drew to the end of his earthly days he could say to his enemies, 'Can any of you prove me guilty of sin?' (John 8:46). Nobody had anything to say. He could say of his Father, 'I always do what pleases him' (John 8:29). What a contrast between our sinful world, steeped in sin, reeking in its sin, on the one hand, and Jesus, the sinless one, on the other.

(2) *Love instead of a calloused spirit.* Or again, what a contrast there was between that holy child and the calloused world outside. To be calloused means to be hard, not to care, to have no sensitivity for other people. But when you look at that child and realise who he is – Immanuel, God

156

with us – you realise that he is the very opposite of being calloused. Even as a baby he speaks to us of a loving, giving, generous, compassionate God, because it was in Jesus that God was reaching out to save us from sin.

(3) *Drawing together rather than dividing.* Or again, what a contrast between that hopelessly divided world and Jesus. If anyone ever had it all together, as we say, it was Jesus. And if anyone ever brought the world together, it was Jesus. He brought it together in all sorts of ways, every way you can think of. He brought God and man together in his Person, because he was the God-man. He had to be the God-man to be our Saviour. He brought time and eternity together, because he is the timeless one. He is the everlasting God, the ancient of days, who nevertheless entered time.

And not only did Jesus bring God and man together in his Person and time and eternity together by his incarnation, he also joined us who are sinners to the Father by his death for us. His death bridged the great gulf that exists between ourselves and God because of sin.

Moreover, where Jesus has done that, he bridges all other divisions that mar our existence. He has created one new people for himself, giving us new natures so that we now read, 'There is neither Jew nor Greek, slave nor free, male nor female, for [we] are all one in Christ Jesus' (Gal. 3:28).

(4) *Joy rather than sorrow.* The final contrast was between the sad world outside and the joy that was present in the stable. There was joy in the birth itself, of course. The birth of a child is usually joyful. The picture of Mary, Joseph and the baby in the manger is a joyful picture. But there was especial joy on this occasion, because this child who was born was the Son of God.

This was the one for whom the people of God had waited down through the long centuries of ancient Jewish history. Adam had waited for that Son, because God had told him that one would be born from the seed of the woman who would crush Satan's head. Yet Adam did not see him. Abraham waited for him. Abraham's children waited. David waited. Isaiah waited. All the prophets waited. But it was not until the day of the last of the prophets, John the Baptist, that Jesus Christ was made known. And here he was in that stable. What a joyful, joyful thing it was! No wonder the angel told the shepherds, 'I bring you good news of great joy that will be for all the people' (Luke 2:10) and the heavenly host broke forth in praise to God, singing,

'Glory to God in the highest,
    and on earth peace to men on whom his favour
    rests' (v. 14).

Through New Eyes
There is only one other thing I want you to see. We have noticed how the shepherds went through the city of Bethlehem, seeing it for what it was. When they came to the manger they saw a great contrast. I do not know how long they stayed near the manger, but eventually they had to leave. And when they left the manger to go back to their fields and their sheep, of necessity they passed through the town again. It was the same town. It was the same sinful, calloused, divided, sad city. In a certain sense, they must have perceived it to be even more sinful, more calloused, more divided and sadder than when they had come in. Having looked into the face of Jesus Christ, they must have seen it for what it really was.

Yet when they had left the manger and went back into the world, they must also have seen the city in a transformed light. It was indeed worse than they had imagined. But together with seeing it from God's point of view, they must have also begun to see it as a world God deeply loved and for which he was now sending his own beloved Son to die. 'For God so loved the world that he gave his one and only Son' (John 3:16).

Love that world? That sinful, evil, wretched, God-hating, man-destroying world? Yes, God loved that world.

That world? That calloused, cruel, hard, indifferent world? A world so insensitive it would not even make a place for Mary who was about to give birth? A world that would crucify Jesus? Yes, God loved that world.

That world? That divided, angry, warring, conspiring, prejudiced world? A world where people hate those who are not like themselves, where nations conspire against other nations and even work to eradicate other races if they can? Yes, God loved that world.

That world? That sad, grey, dismal, pathetic, miserable, dying world? Yes, God loved the world so much that he gave his Son to die for it.

I am sure that what happened is that, having seen Jesus and having, therefore, begun to see the world in God's way, the shepherds went out into that world and began to regard it a little more like God did. How do we know? We know because we are told that they 'spread the word concerning what had been told them about this child' (v. 17). They began to say, 'The Saviour of the world has been born. The hope of the world has come.'

All this would just be an agreeable mental exercise if it were merely something in the past with no bearing upon us. But it has a very direct bearing on us because, as I have tried to show, the world of Bethlehem, Judea, Greece and Rome – that wretched, ancient, sinful world – is our world too. It is the world in which we live, and that baby was the Christ we have come to believe in and worship. His very name means 'Saviour'.

So when you are out in the world this Christmas, when you are doing your shopping and people are pushing you aside – when you are trying to park and there are no places and everybody is blowing his horn at everybody else, where it is dangerous even to cross the street because the drivers are so angry they are likely to run down pedestrians who do not wait for them, when you get in the stores and nobody will wait on you because they are all too tired and hassled, and harsh words are spoken, and when the joy of the season is a joke – try seeing the world as those who have first seen Jesus.

You will find that the world is everything bad you imagined it to be, and worse. It is sinful, hard, divided, sad, but it is the world for whom Jesus came, and he is its Saviour. If you know him as your Saviour, love the world and tell people about him. The world desperately needs to hear that message.

PART FOUR

COMING TO JESUS

13

'WHERE IS HE?'

(Matthew 2:1, 2)

After Jesus was born in Bethlehem in Judea, during the time of King Herod, Magi from the east came to Jerusalem and asked, 'Where is the one who has been born king of the Jews? We saw his star in the east and have come to worship him.'

In the first of his letters to the Christians at Corinth the Apostle Paul wrote that 'not many ... wise [men] by human standards, not many who are influential, not many ... of noble birth' have been chosen by God to know Christ (1 Cor. 1:26). True enough!

But there are some.

The Christmas story tells us that from the beginning of the Christian era there have been some who *were* wise, some who *were* of noble birth, some who *were* influential who came to Jesus. We call them the Wise Men or Magi. They came from the distant east, probably Persia, and they were so distinguished even by the worldly standards of that day that their arrival in Jerusalem created a great stir. 'King Herod ... was disturbed, and all Jerusalem with him' (v. 3). They came asking, 'Where is the one who has been born king of the Jews? We saw his star in the east and have come to worship him' (v. 2).

The coming of the wise men teaches us important things: (1) that God calls the great of this world as well as the seemingly insignificant; (2) that he calls Gentiles as well as Jews.

But the thing I want you to see most forcefully in this study is that, although it is God alone who calls (and calls effectively), nevertheless we must come seeking. God called the Wise Men; the appearance of the star alone teaches that. But they were seekers nonetheless. They sought Jesus, asking everyone, 'Where is the one who has been born king of the Jews?'

An Urgent Question

In recent years Bible translators have pointed out that 'Wise Men' is not the best way to translate the Greek word *magoi*, which is what the text in Matthew uses. They prefer the more literal rendering Magi, thereby rightly identifying the Wise Men as part of the priestly ruling class of Persia at this time. The word *magoi* actually means 'the great (or powerful) ones,' and it is used of them because of their great influence. All this is true. Nevertheless, these were truly wise men, as the story shows, and we are wise to remember that they were and learn from them.

I find several ways in which these men were wise.

First, they were wise to know that, although they had been informed of the birth of this new king of the Jews, they still did not know who or where he was. They were wise enough to ask for him. They asked everyone. I notice that the story does not say that the Wise Men asked their question first of Herod. They did not meet Herod until halfway through the story. Still they were asking after Jesus, and this means that they were probably asking everyone in every possible place and with a commendable persistence that refused to be denied.

I suppose they asked first at the gate of the city as they arrived with their large entourage of servants, camp-followers and guards. They asked the soldiers who were defending the city's entrance, 'Where is he? Where is the one who has been born king of the Jews?'

When the soldiers did not know they must have pressed their questions upon the common citizens and passers-by. 'Where is the one who has been born king of the Jews?'

Later they would have asked the priests, Pharisees and Herodians. At last news of their arrival and questions reached the palace, and Herod himself was greatly disturbed by it.

Wise Enough to Learn

Here is another way in which the Magi were wise. They were wise enough to learn from others, even though there was little information to be had from either the people or their leaders. These were wise men, after all. In their own country they were the ones from whom others sought information. They were the intellectuals of their culture. They had the Ph.D.s. But here they seek more information, standing meekly as genuine disciples when the chief priests and teachers of the law in Jerusalem opened the Scriptures and read to them from the minor prophet Micah:

> But you, Bethlehem, in the land of Judah, are by no means least among the rulers of Judah; for out of you will come a ruler who will be the shepherd of my people Israel (v. 6; from Micah 5:2).

What they learned as the Scriptures were opened to them was important. They learned that Christ was to be born in Bethlehem, a nearby town, and because they were wise they must have understood that this was as significant for what it did not say as for what it did. We must suppose that the Magi were expecting to find the Lord Jesus Christ in Jerusalem, for that was the capital city and Jesus was the Jews' king. They probably expected him to be found in Herod's palace. But he was not there. In fact, the reigning king did not even know about his birth.

Not in the palace? Well, then, perhaps in the temple. Perhaps the new spiritual leader would be there. But Jesus was not to be found in the temple either. He had not emerged from the company of the priests or scribes. On the contrary, his place of birth was the little town of Bethlehem to the south of Jerusalem, an apparently insignificant spot, where the Scriptures had long ago indicated he would be born.

The Wise Men learned that as they listened to the teachers of the law.

I note that these teachers of the law, the scribes, were themselves unworthy men, who had so little interest in the birth of Israel's Messiah that they did not even accompany the eastern kings to Bethlehem to try and find him for themselves. But that did not matter to the Wise Men, because God was calling the Wise Men to Christ, and his call together with their seeking would in due time surely lead them to him. Their quest was so serious, their questions so earnest, that they were able to learn both from those who did not know where he was (the masses of the city) as well as from those, like the chief priests and teachers of the law, who knew but did not care.

I wish there were more people who sought the Lord Jesus Christ like this today. It is true that there are significant obstacles to be overcome.

There is the obstacle of great distance. We are all far from him because of our sin.

There is the obstacle of ignorance. Few know where he may be found. There are even false teachers to throw us off the course.

There is the very great obstacle of indifference. Most people do not care where Jesus is. They do not give him even a casual thought.

But these obstacles, though real, are never a sufficient deterrent for those whom God is calling to faith in Christ. The ones God is calling....

Travel any distance,

Cross any stretch of intellectual desert,

Bridge any chasm of tradition to find Jesus. And they do not stop until their quest is satisfied.

I wish there were many more of them.

Of course, the reason many do not find Jesus is that they are not truly seeking him. This is because, although we are far from him because of our sin, he is not far from us. In one of his sermons on this text Charles Haddon Spurgeon wrote,

> Usually in going up to God's house we get what we go for. Some come because it is the custom, some to meet a friend, some they scarce know why. But when you know what you come for, the Lord who gave you the desire will gratify it... When a sinner is very hungry after Christ, Christ is very near to him. The worst of it is, many of you do not come to find Jesus, it is not him you are seeking for. If you were seeking him, he would soon appear to you.
>
> A woman was asked during a revival, 'How is it you have not found Christ?'
>
> 'Sir,' said she, 'I think it is because I have not sought him.' It is so. None shall be able to say at the last, 'I sought him, but I found him not.' In all cases at the last, if Jesus is not found, it must be because he has not been devotedly, earnestly, importunately sought,

for his promise is, 'Seek, and ye shall find.' These Wise Men are to us a model in many things, and in this among the rest – that their motive was clear to themselves, and they avowed it to others.

May all of us seek Jesus that we may worship him.[1]

A Second Question

The answer to the Wise Men's first question was an encouraging one. They asked, 'Where is the one who has been born king of the Jews?' and they were told (although it was not what they expected) that the child was near at hand, in Bethlehem to the south.

But at this point I imagine that they may have had another question. King Herod had received them. He had produced a technical answer to their question. He had even charged them to 'make a careful search for the child' and to report back to him when they had found him. But as the Wise Men left his presence to go to Bethlehem, they must have been asking, 'But how are we to find him in Bethlehem? We are strangers here. We will be even stranger there. Besides, even though Bethlehem must be a much smaller city than Jerusalem, still it must have many people and many families. How are we to find one special child among so many?'

The answer to the Wise Men's question was the reappearance of the star. God would guide them.

God would lead the Magi to the Saviour.

I do not want to spend much time speculating on the nature of this star. There have been many attempts to explain it as an astronomical phenomenon. The earliest attempts viewed it as a comet. The great church father Origin of Alexandria was one who did this.

---

[1] Charles Haddon Spurgeon, 'The Sages, the Star and the Saviour' in *The Metropolitan Tabernacle Pulpit*, vol. 16 (Pasadena, Texas: Pilgrim Publications, 1970), p. 714. Original edition 1870.

Later Johannes Kepler, a father of modern astronomy, explained it as the conjunction of two planets, Jupiter and Saturn, in the constellation of Pisces in the year 7 BC. This view has been elaborated in various ways and is probably the favourite explanation of the operators of planetariums today, where the December programmes frequently focus on this part of the Christmas story.

The best view is probably that the 'star' was an appearance of the Shekinah glory that had accompanied the people of Israel in their desert wanderings, signifying God's presence with them. The Shekinah moved about, and only something like this, not a conjunction of planets, could have led the Wise Men over the desert to Jerusalem, reappeared and later have 'stopped over the place where the child was' (v. 9).

Yet, as I say, I am not very much interested in the nature of this star here. The point I want to make is that God effectively leads those who are seeking Jesus Christ. He does so in a variety of ways. Someone has written, 'Omnipotence has servants everywhere.' How true! Therefore, God can lead a person to Jesus not only by a star but by a blade of grass, a smile, a snowflake, a 'chance' meeting, an accident, a stone, a drop of dew – anything at all. And, as a matter of fact, he has.

I think of Brother Lawrence, the humble Carmelite monk who produced the classic Christian devotional book The Practice of the Presence of God. Brother Lawrence was born Nicolas Herman. He started out as a footman and a soldier. But one day, when he was eighteen, his attention was drawn to a tree in winter, stripped of its leaves, standing gaunt against the snow. He began to reflect on the change that spring would bring, as new energy would flow through those apparently dead branches and new growth would appear. These thoughts led him to think of God who is the source of such power, not only for trees but for human beings as well. That tree led Brother Lawrence to Jesus, and he became a Christian.

I think of Saint Augustine who was led to Christ by the singing of a child in the garden of a friend's estate in Milan, Italy. The child sang the Latin words 'tole, lege' (take and read). Augustine followed that lead, picked up a Bible that was lying nearby, read from the twelfth chapter of the book of Romans and was converted.

Malcolm Muggeridge, the well-known British social critic, was converted while walking along the road from Jerusalem to Emmaus. He was in Israel filming a special documentary for British television on the resurrection appearances of Christ to his disciples.

A star. A tree. A song. A road.

It makes no difference to God, who uses these and countless other things as his servants in drawing men and women to Christ.

I know that someone will be saying, 'But surely God uses Scripture to save people. No one finds Jesus apart from the written Word of God.' I am not denying that. Brother Lawrence, Saint Augustine and Malcolm Muggeridge certainly knew Scripture, and they were drawn to it even more as the result of their particular experiences. I would argue that this had even been the case with the Wise Men. They had heard the Word of God in Jerusalem, where the words of Micah were produced by the teachers of the law. But it is also possible (I would argue for it strongly) that they had received something of the Word of God in Persia, if that is where they were from. That is where Daniel had prophesied, and he had been one of the Magi of his day. Were those sacred writings not preserved? Were they not known to these Wise Men? I think they must have been, and if they were, the Wise Men would have possessed prophecies of the coming future ruler of the Jews that are as clear as and more detailed than almost any other Old Testament writing.

God certainly reveals Christ in Scripture. But he also uses a variety of means to catch our attention and point us to the Bible.

I like the way Spurgeon put it:

> The Master-Fisher hath a bait for each one of his elect, and often-times he selects a point in their own calling to be the barb of the hook. Were you busy at your counter? Did you hear no voice saying. 'Buy the truth and sell it not'? When you closed your shop last night did you not bethink yourself that soon you must close it for the last time? Do you make bread? And do you never ask yourself, 'Has my soul eaten the bread of heaven?' Are you a farmer? Do you till the soil? Has God never spoken to you by those furrowed fields and these changing seasons, and made you wish that your heart might be tilled and sown?
>
> Listen! God is speaking! Hear, ye deaf; for there are voices everywhere calling you to heaven. You need not go miles about to find a link between you and everlasting mercy. ... If not among the stars, yet among the flowers of the garden, or the cattle of the hills, or the waves of the sea, may he find a net in which to enclose you for Christ. [2]

A Needless Question

I have spoken of two questions that were (or may have been) asked by the Magi who came to Jerusalem to find Christ: 'Where is the one who has been born king of the Jews' and 'How may we find him?' The first question is explicit in the story. The second is based on the fact that the Wise Men still did not know where he was even after they had been with Herod.

---

[2] Charles Haddon Spurgeon, 'The Star and the Wise Men' in *The Metropolitan Tabernacle Pulpit*, vol. 29 (London: The Banner of Truth Trust, 1971), p. 10. Original edition 1884.

I close with a third question. But I introduce it by saying that it is the one question the Wise Men did not ask, and the reason they did not ask it is that they had asked and answered it even before they set out from their homeland for Jerusalem. 'What shall we do when we find him?' That is the question they had no need to ask, because they had already determined that when they found him they would immediately fall down and worship him and then present to him their gifts of gold, incense and myrrh.

Here we touch on a problem many have: half-hearted commitment to Christ, when he should be found.

Many do not find Jesus because they do not really seek him, as I showed earlier. They see the star, but they do not make the journey. Or they make the journey, but they are not willing to admit their ignorance in spiritual matters and so are not willing to learn about him.

But there is another problem too, and the actions of the Wise Men point to it by contrast. Many have a form of seeking, but they have not determined in advance that when they find Christ they will acknowledge him as Christ, worship him and offer him all they have and are. I will not say that God never draws and wins half-hearted followers. I will not say that a person cannot start out holding something back but nevertheless be won by God so that in the end he or she gives everything freely in Christ's service. But I will say that the surest way of finding Christ is to determine in advance to give all you are to him as soon as you do find him and to hold nothing back.

The best way of finding Jesus is to pray, 'Dear Lord Jesus, I do not yet know where you are or how I may find you. I have followed many false leads, some of which are in my own false heart. I need help if I am to find you. God the Father must lead me to you. I do not even know all that this may mean. But I do promise that if you reveal yourself to me, so that I discover you as my own personal God and Saviour, then I will be yours for ever. I will follow you wherever you may lead, and I will give all I possess, both now and later, in your service.'

If you are not yet a Christian, I urge you to follow after Christ on those terms. Do so with urgency and expectation, for you are not as far away from him as were the Wise Men. You do not have hundreds of miles to travel. You are hearing about him now. For you it is as Paul said to the Athenians: 'God ... is not far from each one of us' (Acts 17:27).

And if you are already a Christian, I urge you to worship Jesus and give him your gifts, as the wise men did. You can never worship him too much. You can never give to him too generously.

'What shall I give?' you ask.

Well, if you have gold, as the Magi did, you may give that. Many have much of this world's wealth and use it wisely to spread the gospel of Christ and thus advance his kingdom in the world.

If you have incense, give incense. Mary of Bethany broke her alabaster jar of incense and poured that out upon Jesus. She was commended for it, for Jesus himself said that her gift would be remembered as a memorial to her throughout all generations (Mark 14:9).

If you have myrrh, give myrrh.

If you have none of these things (or even if you do), be sure to give Jesus your love, for love will unlock the other treasures of your life and heart. If you love him, you will give him your tongue, speaking often about him. If you love him, you will give him your hands, working hard for him. If you love him, you will give him your feet, going where he wants you to go.

In short, you will give him your whole self, and you will show it in everything you do. Because, like the Wise

Men, having found Christ and having been warned by God of those who hate him, you will return another way. You will not be the same person you were before you met him, and you will always show by the way you walk thereafter that you have been with Jesus.

14

FINDING JESUS IN BAD TIMES
(Matthew 2:1-11)

After Jesus was born in Bethlehem in Judea, during the time of King Herod, Magi from the east came to Jerusalem and asked, 'Where is the one who has been born king of the Jews? We saw his star in the east and have come to worship him.' When King Herod heard this he was disturbed, and all Jerusalem with him.

For most of us Christmas is a nostalgic time. We remember our childhood Christmases – the family traditions, trees, presents, parties – and we usually look back on those distant years as particularly happy. Most of us probably do the same thing in our reflections on the first Christmas. We think of it as a beautiful family time – for Mary, Joseph and the child – and we may even glamorise the visit by the Magi.

But, of course, it was not a good time. The age that witnessed the birth of Jesus Christ was a bad age, and it is against the evil black background of these days that the wonder of the coming of Jesus and the discovery of him by the Magi should be seen.

Most periods of ancient history were bad in the sense that life was hard for nearly everyone. For most people it was difficult merely to survive. No one but the very few had money. Food was scarce. Usually there was some corrupt king or power to threaten life itself. Bad? Almost always! But life was particularly bad in Judah during the later years of the reign of Herod the Great, the 'monster' of the Christmas story.[1]

The early days of Herod's thirty-three year reign had been notable for such things as a relatively stable government, increase in trade, and many exceptional building projects, particularly the construction of the great golden temple in Jerusalem. But Herod was disliked by his subjects. He was only a half-Jew to begin with, and he relied heavily on Rome, which was perceived as a hostile, pagan power. As a result, Herod grew increasingly paranoid and cruel in his later years. He was so jealous of his favourite wife that on two occasions he left orders that she was to be killed if he failed to return from some dangerous engagement. Then he finally killed her anyway, as well as her grandfather, mother, brother-in-law, and three of his sons, plus hundreds of his subjects.

Caesar Augustus, who also figures in the Christmas story, observed once that he would rather be Herod's pig than his son. It was a clever remark, depending on the similar-sounding Greek words for 'pig' (*choiros*) and 'son' (*huios*). But it also referred to the fact that the Jews did not kill pigs in order to eat pork.

No, they were not good times when Jesus was born to Mary in far-off Judea in the days of King Herod. They were days of poverty, deprivation, danger, disease and oppression. They were very bad times. But it was in precisely these times that the Wise Men came to Judea and, after a careful and diligent search, found Jesus.

---

[1] Paul L. Maier, 'The Monster of the First Christmas' in *First Christmas* (San Francisco: Harper & Row, 1971), pp. 83-88.

A Hostile King

It was not only the outward circumstances that made these bad times, however. Even more significant than these outward matters was the attitude of the people involved. The first bad attitude was Herod's.

Herod was hostile. True, he did not show his hostility, at least at first. He had not survived the many decades of palace intrigue by being transparent. So when the Magi arrived from the east asking, 'Where is the one who has been born king of the Jews?' Herod did not show his displeasure by throwing the visitors in prison or even murdering them for speaking of a rival king. He dissembled. He hid his feelings and instead inquired of the priests and teachers of the law the place where the Messiah was to be born. And later he asked the Magi the exact time the star had appeared to them. He told them, 'Go and make a careful search for the child. As soon as you find him, report to me, so that I too may go and worship him' (v. 8).

Why was Herod so interested in these details? The sequel to the story makes this plain. For when the Wise Men did not return to Jerusalem but rather went back to their own country another way, Herod sent soldiers to Bethlehem to kill the male children aged two and under. He must have learned that the star had appeared to the Magi within the preceding two years.

Why was Herod so hostile? He was an old man at this point. He died a very short time after. What did he have to fear from a two-year-old child or infant? Herod feared everything, of course. He feared that the child would become the rallying point for a popular uprising among the people, rebelling against his tyrannous rule much as the peoples of eastern Europe have rebelled against their former Communist governments. Herod also feared dying. Many fear dying, particularly if their lives have been filled with evil acts and cruelty. Most of all, perhaps, Herod must have feared some kind of divine judgment on him for his many sins.

How sad, when the one he feared and was trying to kill had been sent by the Father *to save us from our sins* by dying for us!

Indifferent Priests

The Wise Men had another obstacle in their attempt to find Jesus. It was the indifferent attitude of the priests and teachers of the law. These men were the religious professionals of their day. But like so many of their kind, religion had become a mere business for them. It was something they did. It was how they earned their living. The things of God meant little to these very worldly men.

In my opinion their case is sadder even than Herod's, because, unlike Herod, they possessed and even knew the Scriptures. When Herod called the priests and teachers of the law together, he asked them where the Christ was to be born, and – this is what is so striking – they knew the answer. As far as the story is concerned, we do not get the impression that they had to research the answer, poring over commentaries or reviewing numerous weighty studies of prophecy. On the contrary, the answer was on the tip of their tongues. 'That's easy,' they must have said. 'The answer is in Micah. The place the Messiah is to be born is Bethlehem. Micah wrote,

> But you, Bethlehem, in the land of Judah, are by no means least among the rulers of Judah; for out of you will come a ruler who will be the shepherd of my people Israel (vv. 5, 6).

Yet I am sure you have noticed that although these prominent religious figures had the Scriptures and knew the right answer to Herod's question, they had no interest in the answer themselves. Herod was interested – in a perverse and wicked way. But although the answer concerned the Jewish nation as well as God's promises to bless it through the rule of a righteous Shepherd-King in future days, the priests were not interested enough to send a representative down the very short road to Bethlehem to investigate the alleged birth of the Messiah for themselves.

Looking For Jesus Today
What I am going to say in this study is that the Magi did eventually find Jesus in spite of these difficulties. But before I do that, I want to suggest that the troubles they encountered in their bad times are not much different from the troubles you may be encountering in our equally bad times today. We do not have hostile political figures to contend with or even indifferent ministers or priests necessarily. But if you have been seeking Jesus, as I hope you have, I am sure you have encountered the bad attitudes Herod and the priests represented, perhaps even more widely.

I know you have encountered hostility, because the world has always been hostile to God and his Anointed. Apart from the supernatural work of God in a person's life, no one wants God to take over the rule of his life, any more than Herod wanted Jesus to take over his throne. No matter that the Messiah would do the job better! No matter that the reign of God's King was prophesied to be a time of peace as well as an age of spiritual and even material blessing! Herod resisted Jesus' rule for one reason only. He wanted to rule himself. In the same way, the world today also wants to rule itself, even if it does it badly. We each want to do things 'my way'.

According to Psalm 2, the kings and rulers of the earth take their stand against the Lord and his Anointed One, saying, 'Let us break their chains and throw off their fetters' (vv. 2, 3). The world is always at war with the Almighty.

So you won't find help in your search for Jesus from the world. In fact, the opposite is the case. The world will set up every possible barrier to your finding him – personal ambition, ridicule, pleasure, the fast track to economic and professional success, and fame, not to mention a vast variety of religious options, if you must be religious.

'Don't be religious,' your friends will say. 'That's not cool. But if you must be religious, why not try transcendental meditation or yoga or even crystals? Anything but Jesus! Because if you get into this Jesus business, you will find that you are going to have to change your way of living. You won't be fun any more. You'll become serious about things. You will have to serve God.'

The world is accurate in that at least. It knows that being a Christian will make a difference to how one lives.

Maybe you have come far enough in your search to have realised that the world is not friendly to those who are searching for Jesus. So you may have turned to the religious professionals. Is it possible that you have even been hindered here?

It is not always the case. We know that in the days of the indifferent priests who attended Herod's court, there were also godly priests. Luke tells of Zechariah, who was the father of John the Baptist. He was a priest and a godly man. There was also Anna, a prophetess, and other such devout people as Elizabeth and Simeon. Nor can we forget Joseph or Mary, the child's mother. There were significant numbers of genuinely godly people. Yet, sad to say, the majority of the priests and teachers were as uninterested in the Saviour as they might have been if he were only a common peasant who had no significance for them whatever.

I know people whose ministers or priests are in this category. They have found them to be interested in many things – social work, politics, bigger and better church buildings, aesthetics – but not in helping them find Jesus.

Finding Jesus

Christmas is not a sad story, however. It is a joyful story, and the joy in the story is that the Magi in the end did find what they were seeking. They found Jesus, and, as the story says, 'They bowed down and worshipped him' (v. 11).

How did they find him? Or to put it another way, why was their search successful? The answer is that they found Jesus in exactly the way everybody else who has ever found Jesus found him: they were led to him by God. The reason their search was successful is that from the very beginning of their journey, when the star first appeared to them, God was in charge of their journey and was leading them to Jesus step by step.

You are probably aware of some of the theories that have been created to explain the star. Every eight hundred and five years the planets Jupiter and Saturn come very close together, and a year after that Mars also joins this infrequent figuration. This happened in the years 7 and 6 BC. If the Magi were astrologers, which is what the word Magi usually suggests, they would have been watching the sky and would have noticed this unusual display. Add to this that Jupiter was called 'the King's Planet' and that Saturn was associated with the territory of Palestine, and you have a possible explanation of what the star may have been. Unfortunately for this theory, Jupiter, Saturn and Mars never come together entirely, and, of course, they do not move over land to mark a particular place or city.

The last objection also affects two other theories: (1) that the star was a comet or (2) a super-nova. There were several sightings of comets in the years preceding Jesus's birth, and one (described as 'without a tail') may have been an exploding star or nova. But neither would explain how Wise Men from the east would be led to Judah and eventually to Bethlehem.

The best explanation is probably that God sent an otherwise unexplainable celestial sign to guide the Magi.

But here is the important point. It is not what the star was; otherwise God would have told us about it. The point is that God sent the star to guide them. Here it was a star. In the case of the shepherds it was angels. Luke relates how aged Simeon was led to the temple 'by the Spirit' at the time Joseph and Mary were bringing Jesus for the required presentation (Luke 2:27). People have been led to Christ in many thousands of ways – by a word, a book, a gospel tract, a radio or television message, a frightening experience in their lives, a sickness, the death of a friend, a testimony, above all by preaching and by being directed to the Bible and by reading it. But the important thing is that God is behind these means of grace, and it is because he is and has been working in them that Jesus has been found. Salvation is of the Lord! It is his work. That is why you can be encouraged in your search, if you are seeking Jesus.

The Bible says, 'Ask and it will be given you; seek and you will find; knock and the door will be opened to you. For everyone who asks receives; he who seeks finds; and to him who knocks, the door will be opened' (Matt. 7:7, 8). That is true whether these are good times or bad.

Ask, Seek, Knock
Have you ever noticed the large number of Bible verses that encourage us to seek God and promise that we will find him if we seek?

Isaiah 55:6-7: 'Seek the Lord while he may be found; call on him while he is near. Let the wicked forsake his way and the evil man his thoughts. Let him turn to the Lord, and he will have mercy on him, and to our God, for he will freely pardon.'

Jeremiah 29:13: 'You will seek me and find me when you seek me with all your heart.'

Zephaniah 2:3: 'Seek the Lord, all you humble of the land, you who do what he commands.'

Amos 5:6: 'Seek the Lord and live.'

I am well aware that the Bible also teaches that no one naturally seeks God of himself or herself: 'There is no one who understands, no one who seeks God' (Rom. 3:11). If we find ourselves seeking, it is because God is already working in our lives. But that in itself is an encouragement, and it is why I encourage you, if you are really seeking. If you are seeking Jesus, it is because, as in the case of the Wise Men, God is already leading you to him. I have two more points of encouragement also.

First, although you are seeking him, God has already done the really hard part by bringing Jesus to you. That is what the incarnation is about. The Wise Men probably travelled to Judah from far-distant Babylonia or Persia. But before they had even started out, God had travelled the infinitely greater distance from heaven to earth and from the throne of glory to a stable, that Jesus might be found. God has not remained aloof. He has not played it safe by remaining behind the high ramparts of an unassailable heaven. He has come down to us, to our world, and he has become like us. In one sense, he has become as accessible as our neighbour next-door.

Secondly, I want to encourage you by this. In the story of the Magi, Jesus was found by those who initially were far from him and who, as far as any natural relationships or affinities are concerned, had no share in the Messiah. They came from the east. They were Gentiles and not Jews. They had no Bibles. They probably had many utterly pagan ideas. But because God was working in them, these far-off ones came close and eventually found Jesus. Charles Haddon Spurgeon had a sermon on this theme, entitled, *The Far-Off, Near; the Near, Far Off*, contrasting the Magi, who were from Persia, with Herod and the priests, who were from Judea. Herod and the priests were only a few short miles from Bethlehem, but they did not find Jesus. In the case of the priests, they did not even seek for him. But the Wise Men, who had no natural claim on him and were from far off, found and worshipped Jesus.[2]

Shouldn't you be encouraged by that? It doesn't matter how far off you may think yourself to be – whether because of some sin you have committed or the coldness of your heart or anything else. God delights in calling distant ones to Jesus.

But I have a warning too. It is from Isaiah 55:6, which says, 'Seek the Lord while he may be found' and 'call on him while he is near.' You are encouraged to come. There are ample promises in the Bible to encourage you in your search. But the Bible also says that there are seasons for everything and that the times at which Jesus may be found will not last. They will not last for ever. One day you and I will die, and then the time for our personal repentance and faith in Christ will be past. One day there will be a final judgment. Then it will be too late for everyone. Besides, even in this life there are times when the heart is tender and Jesus is near, followed by times in which the

---

[2] Charles Haddon Spurgeon, 'The Far-off Near; the Near, Far Off' in *The Metropolitan Tabernacle Pulpit*, vol. 39 (Pasadena, Texas: Pilgrim Publications, 1975), p. 433-442.

seed that has been sown seems to be snatched away lest it be allowed to sink down into the heart and bear fruit.

If you are seeking, don't delay your search. Search now, and search 'with all your heart,' which is what Jeremiah says is necessary if you are to be assured of finding Jesus.

In fact, why should your search go any further than this moment? You already know far more than the Wise Men knew, even after they had arrived in Bethlehem. They knew that the child they worshipped was Israel's King. But you know that he is the world's King too. More than that, you know he is the Saviour.

You know that the child grew to be a man who travelled throughout the ancient land of the Jews, teaching about God and saying that he had been sent by God, his Father, to die on a cross and thus make atonement for the sins of all who believe on him. You know that the time came when he did die. The child, now grown, stretched out his hands and was impaled upon a cross, dying in your place, bearing your sin, so that you might not have to suffer for it. All he requires is that you come to him. He demands that you leave your sin and throw yourself completely upon him as your Saviour.

You also know that this Jesus, the one who was born for you and died for you, rose from the dead for you – so that you might not fear the grave but might have the assurance of going to be with him in heaven forever when you die.

Seeking Jesus in bad times?

I suppose ours are bad times, at least as bad as the times in which the Wise Men sought him. But the Wise Men found him. And if that was the case, why should you not find him also? It is the same Jesus, the same God, the same route, the same gospel. Yes, and you are the same too. Your need is the same. And when you have found him, you need to do the same as the Wise Men. You need to bow down and worship him and then present your gifts. You need to present everything you are. And then you need to go home another way, which means living a different life than you have lived before.

15

THOSE WHO LOST CHRISTMAS

(Luke 2:41-52)

Every year his parents went to Jerusalem for the Feast of the Passover. When he was twelve years old, they went up to the Feast, according to the custom. After the Feast was over, while his parents were returning home, the boy Jesus stayed behind in Jerusalem, but they were unaware of it. Thinking he was in their company, they travelled on for a day. Then they began looking for him among their relatives and friends. When they did not find him, they went back to Jerusalem to look for him. After three days they found him in the temple courts, sitting among the teachers, listening to them and asking them questions. Everyone who heard him was amazed at his understanding and his answers. When his parents saw him, they were astonished. His mother said to him, 'Son, why have you treated us like this? Your father and I have been anxiously searching for you.'

'Why were you searching for me?' he asked. 'Didn't you know I had to be in my Father's house?' But they did not understand what he was saying to them.

Then he went down to Nazareth with them and was obedient to them. But his mother treasured all these things in her heart. And Jesus grew in wisdom and stature, and in favour with God and men.

A popular saying about love goes, 'It is better to have loved and lost than never to have loved at all.' That may be true, but what the saying does not acknowledge is that there is pain in having lost something and that the pain would not be there if the object or the person had not been possessed in the first place.

Over the years, as I have prepared messages for Christmas, I have been impressed with those in the story who missed Christmas, on the one hand, or found it, on the other. By 'it' or 'Christmas' I am really speaking about Jesus Christ, the central figure of the story. So when I speak of those who missed, found or (in this study) lost Christmas, I really mean those who missed, found or lost Jesus.

The political leaders of the day missed Christmas. So did the innkeeper and the religious leaders. They were all preoccupied with one thing or another and so missed the greatest event of their lifetimes, the birth of God's Son, the Saviour of the world.

The poor people of the time found Christmas. They were people like the shepherds, who were not very well thought of socially; Anna, an old widow who lived in Jerusalem; and Simon, who actually held the Christ-child in his arms. The Wise Men from the east also found him by following the star God sent to guide them to Bethlehem. I have explored the stories of these people carefully in other sermons.[1]

The story we come to in this study concerns people who found Christmas, who found Christ, but who then lost him. It concerns a trip the holy family made to Jerusalem when Jesus was only twelve years old. It tells how in the bustle and busyness of that trip Jesus was somehow left behind in Jerusalem and how Mary and

---

[1] See 'The Little People of Christmas' and 'Those Who Missed Christmas' in James Montgomery Boice, *The Christ of Christmas* (Chicago: Moody Press, 1983).

Joseph travelled a whole day's journey without knowing that he was missing.

This is something that happens in many people's lives. There was a time in their lives when they were missing what Christianity is about. Then they found Jesus Christ as their Saviour. In those days the joy of their Christian lives was rich, and they were filled with gratitude for all they had found in Jesus. But then, as time went by, there was a period – perhaps you are in something like it now – when the joy of those earlier days seemed to fade away and they entered into what the mystics called the 'dark night of the soul'. Jesus seemed lost, so far as they were concerned. He was not lost, of course. We are the ones who lost him, not he us. But sometimes we lose sight of him, and the life once filled with joy seems empty.

William Cowper, the English poet who composed some of our most moving hymns, described it from his own experience:

> Where is the blessedness I knew
>> When first I saw the Lord?
> Where is the soul-refreshing view
>> Of Jesus and his Word?
>
> What peaceful hours I then enjoyed,
>> How sweet their memory still;
> But now I find an aching void
>> The world can never fill.

If you have experienced or are experiencing that sense of loss now, I want you to think about the lessons found in this story.

Anybody, Any Place

The first thing I notice is that this is an experience that can happen to anybody. Some years ago the evangelist Gypsy Smith preached a sermon on this passage which contained two points: (1) the experience of losing Christ happened to the most unlikely people, and (2) the experience of losing Christ happened in the most unlikely place.

It is hard to imagine anybody who would have had a greater responsibility and a greater desire to hang on to Jesus than his parents, Joseph and Mary. Jesus was an exceptional child, and theirs must have been an exceptional care. Even with our children, though there is much of our sinful nature in them, there are often touches of the work of the Holy Spirit and we are attracted to and encouraged by that spiritual fruit. Think of what this would have been like in the case of Joseph and Mary as Jesus grew up in their home. There was no sin in him whatever. He was filled with all grace and truth. Jesus never lied, never did anything wrong, was always perfectly obedient. Think of raising a child like that. What love, what concern, what affection Mary and Joseph must have had for this child!

Besides, Mary and Joseph had been told that Jesus was to be the world's Saviour, and both knew the miraculous nature of his birth. Jesus' parents must have cared for him as no parents in all history have ever cared for their child. Yet it was these very people, Mary and Joseph, who lost him on this occasion.

They also lost him in the most unlikely place, Jerusalem. If they had been visiting pagan cities or parts of Jerusalem where the lowest types of people hung out, we could understand how they might have lost Jesus. He might have said, 'I'm not going to go in there. That is not a good environment for me.' It is true that later Jesus did go to such places to seek those who were lost. But at this point in his life, if he had been taken there and had refused to enter such an evil place, we could understand how Mary and Joseph might have lost him.

Or again, if they had been attending a school of the philosophers and if they had been attracted by the new learning of the day or had been enamoured of the new morality, we can understand how they might have lost Jesus there. He could have said, 'I must be about my Father's business. This is not the place for me.' But that was not the case either. The holy family was in Jerusalem. This was the Feast of the Passover, the great feast of Israel, and they were there to worship God in the company of God's people. It was in such a setting, not a bad setting, that they somehow lost Jesus and started home unaware that he was not with them.

If this could happen to Mary and Joseph in a place like Jerusalem, you and I can certainly lose the sense of the presence of Christ wherever we may be. This can happen in many places. Sadly it can happen even in church and in the fellowship of God's people. We can find ourselves drifting spiritually, and we can enter into a period where all that seemed rich, wonderful and glorious fades away and we even find ourselves wondering if what we had experienced before was real at all. The first time that happens to Christians many tend to say, 'Well, it just wasn't real; I wasn't saved in the first place.' Generally they were. But these experiences can still happen, and they can still be very painful.

Our Own Understanding
The second thing I want to look at is the problem. And I want to ask: Why did it happen? I think there is a clue in verse 44, which says, 'Thinking he was in their company, they travelled on for a day.' That is an accurate translation of what the Greek text says, but I prefer the translation of the King James Bible which, at this point, is no less accurate but adds, I think, a dimension that the word 'thinking' does not. The King James Version says, 'Supposing him to be in their company....' Supposing involves thinking, naturally, but it also suggests inaccurate imaginings, that

191

is, thinking that to be so which is not actually so. This was the case with Mary and Joseph. They were trusting their supposings when they had not actually made certain where the Lord was.

This is what is wrong in the lives of many people. They suppose (or trust to their own reasoning), and so depart from the Scriptures and enter into an intellectual and spiritual morass.

This has happened historically. It is very interesting how in the history of New Testament criticism, particularly in regard to the many books written on the life of Jesus during the nineteenth century, people on the basis of their own suppositions drifted further and further from who the true Christ is. By the time they had finished they often had no Christ at all.

That famous book by Albert Schweitzer, *The Quest for the Historical Jesus*, was a masterpiece of analytical research. Schweitzer analysed the books on the life of Jesus that had been written during the nineteenth century, showing how their authors began by weeding out the things they did not think appropriate or believable about Christ and eventually reconstructed Jesus as they thought he should be. But what happened, as Schweitzer so thoroughly pointed out, is that they simply reconstructed Jesus in their own image. Idealists produced an idealistic Jesus. Rationalists produced a Jesus who was a great teacher of morality. Socialists produced a socialistic Jesus. The most popular books written on the life of Jesus, those by David Friedrich Strauss, ended by discounting much of the gospels as mythology, something in which people today cannot believe. And at the end of that period, along came Bruno Bauer who denied that there had even been a historical Jesus.

This is what happens when people follow their suppositions and departs from the text of Scripture where alone we learn who Jesus really is.

I wish it could be said that what happened in the nineteenth century taught scholars a lesson and that the errors have been laid to rest for ever by Schweitzer's book. But that is not the case. In our time we have had a number of equally silly and far less well-documented books on the life of Christ: *The Passover Plot* and *The Sacred Mushroom and the Cross*, to give just two examples. *The Passover Plot* supposed that the crucifixion was designed by Jesus to imitate what he supposed the Messiah should have done. He was to be crucified, then be rescued by his friends and pretend to be resurrected. According to this book, Jesus actually died by accident due to the unanticipated spear-thrust of the Roman soldier. Even more ludicrous is *The Sacred Mushroom* which tries to explain the origins of Christianity by imagining the existence of an ancient drug cult from which the Christian religion is supposed to have come.

All this is utterly wrong-headed. The Jesus who existed is the Jesus of the Scriptures. So when we find ourselves imagining or supposing who Jesus Christ is, apart from the Scriptures, we are starting off in a direction that actually takes us from him. The book of Proverbs says, 'Trust in the Lord with all your heart and lean not on your own understanding; in all your ways acknowledge him, and he will make your paths straight' (Prov. 3:5, 6). That is what we need to do. We should come to the Bible, saying, 'Almighty God, I do not trust my own understanding in this, although I will use my reason in every proper way. But I lean on you. Teach me. I am reading your book, the Bible, to hear what you will tell me about your Son.'

There is one other thought here. Not only did Mary and Joseph lose Jesus by their suppositions, suppositions which were divorced from fact. They also lost him by their own carelessness. It is easy to understand how they might have grown careless about Jesus. He was an ideal son. He had always obeyed them, never got into trouble, never did anything wrong. If ever anybody could be trusted, it was Jesus. Perhaps over the years as they saw him develop, Mary and Joseph grew careless where Jesus was concerned.

I notice too that the time at which they lost him was the Passover. It was at the Passover feast. Not a funeral. Not at some other grim period of life. It was a time of joyous celebration.

Charles Haddon Spurgeon preached a number of sermons on this particular portion of Luke's gospel, and in one of them he called attention to the danger of losing Jesus in joyful times. He said:

> I never lost my Master's company at a funeral; such a thing is more than possible at a wedding. I never lost my Saviour's presence in the house of mourning, by the bedside of the sick and dying; but I have sometimes felt suspension of fellowship with my Lord when the lute and the viol have been sounding in my ear, and when joy and gladness ruled the hour. Our happy moments are our most perilous ones.[2]

This is why losing Christ can so easily happen at Christmas when, caught up in the joy of the holidays, the delight of seeing friends or the pleasure of giving and receiving, we somehow forget him who is our true friend and the greatest gift of all.

Back To Jesus
What is to be done if that has happened? There is only one thing to be done. You have to go back to where you lost

---

[2] Charles Haddon Spurgeon, 'A Lost Christ Found' in *The Metropolitan Tabernacle Pulpit*, (Pasadena, Texas: Pilgrim Publications, 1977), vol. 45, p. 99.

Jesus. That is what his parents did. They had travelled for a day. But when they began looking for him among their relatives and friends and did not find him, they went back to Jerusalem to seek him out. That is where they had seen him last. So that is where they went.

This is what you have to do if you have lost the presence of Christ in your life. Where is it that you lost him? You know where that is. It may be that you lost him in your prayer life. There was a time when your prayers were fervent. You were faithful in prayer in those days, and as you think back to them you remember how wonderful those times of prayer were. It was as though you were walking in heaven when you were on your knees. Yet as the days went by and the pressures of life closed in, those times got shorter, and when you did pray your mind was not entirely on what you were saying. Eventually it seemed as if Jesus was no longer there. If that is where you lost him, you must go back and re-establish those times of prayer. You must cry out for him whose presence alone makes life worth living.

Perhaps you lost Jesus at the point of some sin. For you can either have Christ and give up the sin, or you can keep the sin and give up Christ. Christ will not tolerate sin. If you have kept the sin, you know what it is. You know that fork in the road where Jesus was going ahead of you in one direction and sin was beckoning from another. You said, 'Well, I'll just go down this other fork for awhile.' You thought, 'It won't be long; it won't be far. After I go a little way, I'll turn around and come back. I'll be with Jesus again.'

But you never did go back. Sin captured you and led you on from sin to sin. You followed it instead of being led forward from faith to faith as you should have been. If that is the case, that is the point to which you must go back. You must go back to that sin, confess and relinquish it, and then turn again and go in God's way. Blessing will not come back into your life until that turning around has taken place.

Again, maybe you have lost Jesus at the point of your study of the Scriptures. You know that it is through the Word of God that Christians grow. It is by the 'pure spiritual milk' of the Word that babies in Christ become strong (1 Pet. 2:2). It is the 'solid food' of the Word that makes those who are strong grow even stronger (Heb. 5:11-14). It is by Bible study that a Christian resists temptations. The psalmist said, 'I have hidden your word in my heart that I might not sin against you' (Ps. 119:11). But you began to neglect Bible study. You thought, 'I know so many things about the Bible that I no longer need to feed upon the Word of God daily. What I know will stay with me.' Then you drifted further and further away, and now as you think back, you can hardly remember the last time you sat down and studied the Bible seriously.

Does that describe your case? If it is, you need to get back to serious Bible study. You need to search out the mind of God, and when you have found it you need to conform your life to that teaching.

Seek Him While He May Be Found
Let me encourage you as you seek to find the Lord once again. You may have gone a long, long way from Jesus and have lost him for a very long time. Mary lost him for three days: the lost day travelling home, the day returning to Jerusalem, and the day spent searching for him in Jerusalem. Those three days must have seemed like an eternity to Mary. Three days without her son. Lost in Jerusalem, that big city. Whatever had become of him? She must have been in utter distress. But although she was distressed, Mary nevertheless kept her mind about her and sought him and kept on seeking him until

at the end of the three days she held him in her arms again.

What about you? You may have lost Jesus for a longer time than that. It may be three months rather than three days, or even three years. Aren't you distressed? Don't you want to find Jesus again?

However far you have strayed and however long it has been, if you will determine to seek Christ, you will find that he is there to be found. He is not hiding. He said, 'Come to me.' He wants to be found by you. Moreover, when you find him you will find him to be the same gracious, loving, merciful, wise and sovereign Saviour he has always been.

I make this last point.

Almost everything I have said thus far has been for Christians, those who have known the joy of salvation but for one reason or another have lost that joy. But perhaps you have never found Jesus in the first place. What am I to say to you? Your case is exceedingly desperate, the more so because you do not even know what you have lost. A Christian may at least know what he is missing. But what do I say to someone who does not even know what it is to have Christ, to be a child of God and to belong to the blessed company of God's people? Paul said of the Ephesians before the gospel of Christ came to them, 'You were separate from Christ, [and because they were separated from Christ] excluded from citizenship in Israel and foreigners to the covenants of the promise, without hope and without God in the world' (Eph. 2:12). That is an apt description of your spiritual condition. It is a desperate one.

But remember that Jesus came to earth to die for sinners just like yourself, and that he has invited everyone, including yourself, to come to him. Let God's description of your case awaken you from your spiritual danger and lethargy. Let Jesus' invitation stir your heart and get you moving towards him. And may you seek the Lord Jesus Christ, searching diligently, while he can be found.

Other Books of interest
from
Christian Focus Publications

Characters Around The
CRADLE

'This excellent book makes the Passion come alive...'
Joel Edwards

Tom Houston

Characters Around The Cradle

Tom Houston

Christmas makes people both happy and frustrated, especially Christian people. There is a tug-of-war between the secular Christmas with its tinsel, glitter and high spending on gifts, and the meaning it was supposed to have from the unusual birth of Jesus.

Tom Houston looks at a great story with a great cast. The political forces of Caesar Augustus, Herod and the travellers from the east, the religious establishment in Zechariah, Elizabeth, Anna and Simeon, The outcast prophet - John the Baptist, the ordinary people - Mary, Joseph and the shepherds and also the Gospellers - Matthew and Luke.

'Read Characters Around the Cradle and Christmas will live for you in a new way. Perhaps as never before you will realize that the Christmas story was a real happening that can make a difference in your real life today!'

Leighton Ford, President, Leighton Ford Ministries

'Christmas always stirs the imagination, but Tom Houston stirs the readers with reflections from the real biblical characters who surrounded the birth of Jesus... A lively read that warms the heart.'

Chris Wright, Langham Partnership International

Tom Houston served as a pastor for 20 years in Scotland and Kenya and then went on to serve in leadership positions with the British and Foreign Bible Society, World Vision and the Luasanne Committee for World Evangelisation until his retirement in 1994.

ISBN 978-1-85792-755-9

ALEX MACDONALD

TELL ME THE STORY

THE CARPENTER

Tell Me the Story:

The Carpenter

Alex MacDonald

Alex retells these eye-witness stories of Jesus. These people tell their stories as eye witnesses of those who were actually there. They are:

Mary, mother of Jesus, Gaius Maximus, centurion, Joanna's story of John The Baptist, woman at the well, Simon the Pharisee, Gadarene Demoniac, Jairus, Simon Peter, Rich ruler, Bartimaeus & Zacchaeus, John and Marcellus a Roman officer.

Using Biblical, contemporary and background data, Alex MacDonald skilfully tells the stories of those who were with Jesus at key points in his life.

It unfolds as if you were on the spot looking on. The stories are based on factual evidence of what really happened. This book will capture your imagination causing you to ask "What would my reaction have been if I had been there?" or "Was this really what happened"?

'In this book Alex MacDonald retells the story of 12 people who were eyewitnesses to the life of Jesus. The style of the book is compelling and biblical and background material is helpful. The author is an engaging storyteller and manages to captivate heart, mind and imagination of the reader. The book is an easy read...I would certainly give this book to an unbeliever to whet their appetite for the gospel'

Evangelicals Now

Alex MacDonald is the minister of Buccleuch & Greyfriars Free Church of Scotland, Edinburgh

ISBN 978-1-84550-285-0

FELLOWSHIP FAITH
DEVIL REGENERATION
DEATH **18 WORDS**
MEDIATOR ELECTION
GRACE RECONCILIATION

THE MOST IMPORTANT WORDS
YOU WILL EVER KNOW LORD
MORTIFICATION
SANCTIFICATION
HOLINESS JUSTIFICATION
J. I. PACKER
WORLD SIN SCRIPTURE
REVELATION

18 Words:

The most important words you will ever know

J. I. Packer

If the modern world can be characterised by one thing it is probably the enormous increase in the number of words around - but that increase has also been accompanied by a seemingly corresponding decrease in understanding. It is the irony of the information age that instead of bringing clarity it has raised uninformed opinion to the same level as truth.

The church has also not been faultless. Rather than discuss ideas in order to come to some settled agreement, the church has been characterised as trying to make words mean different things in order to accommodate differences.

But the church should be a beacon of light to the world. The church has the words of eternal life.

J. I. Packer is a master wordsmith. He is also gifted with the ability of showing where truth lies in complicated reasoning. These skills combine to make **Words from God** a fascinating read – and a life-changing one.

The 18 words are Death, Devil, Election, Faith, Fellowship, Grace, Holiness, Justification, Lord, Mediator, Mortification, Reconciliation, Regeneration, Revelation, Sanctification, Scripture, Sin & World.

Jim Packer is named by Time Magazine as one of the 25 most influential evangelicals alive. He is the Board of Governor's Professor of Theology at Regent College, Vancouver, BC, Canada.

ISBN 978-1-84550-327-7

sure, I believe - so what!

JAMES MONTGOMERY BOICE

learn from the book of james to:
» use your wealth
» control your tongue
» not worry
» reach out to the friendless

Sure I Believe! - So What?

James Montgomery Boice

No matter how enthusiastically we embrace doctrinal teaching it has no real power unless accompanied by action. James Boice tackles key areas of conflict in the Christian's life - avoiding hypocrisy, guarding our tongues using our wealth appropriately, perseverance.

If you really believe then it will show in your life. James is a practical book, too practical in dealing with our own shortcomings, errors and sins! And it is so direct that we cannot easily dismiss or escape from James' teaching. Prepare to be challenged!

'This exposition of James is one of Boice's most practical books and has abiding relevance for Christian men and women today. Readers will gain a richer understanding of what it means to have a faith that really works.'

Philip Graham Ryken,
Senior Minister, Tenth Presbyterian Church, Philadelphia

'James Boice was one of the greatest Bible teachers of the twentieth century. This exposition of James is an outstanding help, displaying Boice's penetrating mind and easy to read style. I warmly commend it to pastors and all other Bible students.'

Eric Alexander

ISBN 978-1-85792-095-6

Christian Focus Publications

publishes books for all ages

Our mission statement –

STAYING FAITHFUL

In dependence upon God we seek to help make His infallible Word, the Bible, relevant. Our aim is to ensure that the Lord Jesus Christ is presented as the only hope to obtain forgiveness of sin, live a useful life and look forward to heaven with Him.

REACHING OUT

Christ's last command requires us to reach out to our world with His gospel. We seek to help fulfil that by publishing books that point people towards Jesus and help them develop a Christ-like maturity. We aim to equip all levels of readers for life, work, ministry and mission.

Books in our adult range are published in three imprints.

Christian Focus contains popular works including biographies, commentaries, basic doctrine and Christian living. Our children's books are also published in this imprint.

Mentor focuses on books written at a level suitable for Bible College and seminary students, pastors, and other serious readers. The imprint includes commentaries, doctrinal studies, examination of current issues and church history.

Christian Heritage contains classic writings from the past.

Christian Focus Publications Ltd
Geanies House, Fearn,
Ross-shire, IV20 1TW, Scotland, United Kingdom
info@christianfocus.com

Our titles are available from quality bookstores and
www.christianfocus.com